NOVELL'S

GroupWise™ 5
User's Handbook

SHAWN B. ROGERS and RICHARD H. McTAGUE

NOVELL

PRESS®

Novell Press, San Jose

Novell's GroupWise™ 5 User's Handbook
Published by
Novell Press
2180 Fortune Drive
San Jose, CA 95131
www.idgbooks.com (IDG Books Worldwide Web site)

Library of Congress Catalog Card No.: 96-76247
ISBN: 0-7645-4509-4
Printed in the United States of America
1P/SU/RQ/ZW/FC
Distributed in the United States by IDG Books Worldwide, Inc

Distributed by Macmillan Canada for Canada; by Transworld Publishers Limited in the United Kingdom; by IDG Norge Books for Norway; by IDG Sweden Books for Sweden; by Woodslane Pty. Ltd. for Australia; by Woodslane Enterprises Ltd. for New Zealand; by Longman Singapore Publishers Ltd. for Singapore, Malaysia, Thailand, and Indonesia; by Simron Pty. Ltd. for South Africa; by Toppan Company Ltd. for Japan; by Distribuidora Cuspide for Argentina; by Livraria Cultura for Brazil; by Ediciencia S.A. for Ecuador; by Addison-Wesley Publishing Company for Korea; by Ediciones ZETA S.C.R. Ltda. for Peru; by WS Computer Publishing Corporation, Inc., for the Philippines; by Unalis Corporation for Taiwan; by Contemporanea de Ediciones for Venezuela; by Computer Book & Magazine Store for Puerto Rico; by Express Computer Distributors for the Caribbean and West Indies. Authorized Sales Agent: Anthony Rudkin Associates for the Middle East and North Africa.

For general information on IDG Books Worldwide's books in the U.S., please call our Consumer Customer Service department at 800-762-2974. For reseller information, including discounts and premium sales, please call our Reseller Customer Service department at 800-434-3422.

For information on where to purchase IDG Books Worldwide's books outside the U.S., please contact our International Sales department at 415-655-3200 or fax 415-655-3295.

For information on foreign language translations, please contact our Foreign & Subsidiary Rights department at 415-655-3021 or fax 415-655-3281.

For sales inquiries and special prices for bulk quantities, please contact our Sales department at 415-655-3200 or write to the address above.

For information on using IDG Books Worldwide's books in the classroom or for ordering examination copies, please contact our Educational Sales department at 800-434-2086 or fax 817-251-8174.

For press review copies, author interviews, or other publicity information, please contact our Public Relations department at 415-655-3000 or fax 415-655-3299.

For authorization to photocopy items for corporate, personal, or educational use, please contact Copyright Clearance Center, 222 Rosewood Drive, Danvers, MA 01923, or fax 508-750-4470.

John Kilcullen, *President & CEO, IDG Books Worldwide, Inc.*
Brenda McLaughlin, *Senior Vice President & Group Publisher, IDG Books Worldwide, Inc.*
The IDG Books Worldwide logo is a trademark under exclusive license to IDG Books Worldwide, Inc., from International Data Group, Inc.

Rosalie Kearsley, *Publisher, Novell Press, Inc.*
Novell Press and the Novell Press logo are trademarks of Novell, Inc.

Welcome to Novell Press

Novell Press, the world's leading provider of networking books, is the premier source for the most timely and useful information in the networking industry. Novell Press books cover fundamental networking issues as they emerge — from today's Novell and third-party products to the concepts and strategies that will guide the industry's future. The result is a broad spectrum of titles for the benefit of those involved in networking at any level: end-user, department administrator, developer, systems manager, or network architect.

Novell Press books are written by experts with the full participation of Novell's technical, managerial, and marketing staff. The books are exhaustively reviewed by Novell's own technicians and are published only on the basis of final released software, never on prereleased versions. Novell Press at IDG Books Worldwide is an exciting partnership between two companies at the forefront of the knowledge and communications revolution. The Press is implementing an ambitious publishing program to develop new networking titles centered on the current IntranetWare version of NetWare and on Novell's GroupWise and other popular groupware products.

Novell Press books are translated into 12 languages and are available at bookstores around the world.

Rosalie Kearsley, Publisher, Novell, Inc.
David Kolodney, Associate Publisher, IDG Books Worldwide, Inc.

Novell Press

Publisher
Rosalie Kearsley

Associate Publishers
Colleen Bluhm
David Kolodney

Associate Acquisitions Editor
Anne Hamilton

Communications Project Specialist
Marcy Shanti

Executive Managing Editor
Terry Somerson

Development Editor
Ron Hull

Copy Editor
Suki Gear

Technical Editor
Bill Mangum

Editorial Assistants
Sharon Eames
Annie Sheldon

Production Director
Andrew Walker

Production Associate
Christopher Pimentel

Supervisor of Page Layout
Craig A. Harrison

Media/Archive Coordination
Leslie Popplewell
Melissa Stauffer

Project Coordinator
Ben Schroeter

Production Staff
Elizabeth Cárdenas-Nelson
Ritchie Durdin
Craig A. Harrison
Tom Missler

Quality Control Specialist
Mick Arellano

Proofreader
Deborah F. Kaufman
Joel K. Draper

Indexer
Liz Cunningham

Cover Design
Craig Hanson

Cover Photographer
Photonica/Pedro Lobo

Book Design
Kurt Krames

To Kellie and Cameron, for their love, support, and endless patience. Also to my extended family, my Church family, my co-author, and my good friends who continually uplift, strengthen, and encourage me.

Shawn B. Rogers

I dedicate this book to my brother, Scott McTague, who has always shown me the joy and humor in life. He makes me smile when I think about him, and I am extremely proud to be his older brother. Scott, consider this a blatant attempt to get you to move your family to Kansas City, and in the meantime, stay off the trampoline.

Rick McTague

About the Authors

Shawn B. Rogers is the author of *Novell's GroupWise 4 Administrator's Guide* and the co-author of *Novell's GroupWise 4 User's Guide* (both published by Novell Press and IDG Books Worldwide). He is a Senior Instructional Designer for Novell Education. He has four years' teaching experience in GroupWise and other computing technologies. He is also a Certified Novell Engineer (CNE) and a Certified Novell Instructor (CNI) for Novell GroupWise. He lives in Spanish Fork, Utah.

Richard H. McTague is a Messaging Systems Specialist for USConnect Kansas City. He is the co-author of *Novell's GroupWise 4 User's Guide,* and he served as technical editor for *Novell's GroupWise 4 Administrator's Guide.* He has written articles for *Computer User* and *Computing Canada* magazines. He is a CNE and a Certified Novell Instructor (CNI) for Novell GroupWise and Novell NetWare 4.x. He lives in Overland Park, Kansas.

Preface

Welcome to Novell GroupWise 5! GroupWise 5 is Novell's newest version of the most powerful electronic messaging system in the world, and *Novell's GroupWise 5 User's Handbook* will guide you through it. Our goal is to make you productive with GroupWise as quickly as possible. To that end, we only cover the most important features of GroupWise 5 and focus exclusively on the Windows 95 client.

For beginning computer users, this book serves as a guide to get you up and running with GroupWise 5 in minimal time. For more advanced computer users, *Novell's GroupWise 5 User's Handbook* serves as a quick-reference for getting the most out of the GroupWise 5 advanced features.

Keep this book next to the computer where you have GroupWise 5 installed: We provide illustrations of actual GroupWise 5 screens and step-by-step procedures to help you learn the system immediately.

The book is organized as follows:

Chapter 1: Introduction to GroupWise 5

We set out to accomplish two things in this chapter: First, we explain exactly what GroupWise 5 does and how you can use it to increase your productivity. Second, we explain the GroupWise 5 interface. At first glance, the GroupWise 5 interface seems almost too simple to contain all of the information it does. When you finish this section, you will understand how the interface works and how to navigate through GroupWise 5.

Chapter 2: Messaging Fundamentals

In Chapter 2, we explain how to use each of the GroupWise 5 message types and how to send and receive messages. We give step-by-step instructions for sending GroupWise 5 messages and attaching files to messages. We also explain how to read incoming messages, view and save file attachments, print messages, reply to and forward messages, and delete messages.

Chapter 3: Using the GroupWise Address Book

The GroupWise Address Book is a powerful and useful component of GroupWise 5. In Chapter 3, we explain how to use the Address Book to find the addresses of other GroupWise users and how to use the Address Book to send messages to groups of users.

The Address Book can also be used as a personal contact manager. We explain how to create personal contact lists (known as personal address books) and how to add contact records to personal address books.

Chapter 4: Message Management

As you start using GroupWise 5 for everyday work, you will soon experience message overload. Just like a desktop can quickly become cluttered with messages, notes, mail, and paperwork, your GroupWise 5 Mailbox will quickly become unwieldy unless you practice good message management.

In Chapter 4, we explain how to use the GroupWise 5 message management features to prevent message overload. We show you how to find out if someone has opened a message you sent, and we show you how to retract a message when you realize you forgot to attach a file or you forgot to spell-check a message you just sent to the CEO.

We also show you how to set up folders to organize your messages and how to permanently rid yourself of useless messages.

Chapter 5: Personal Calendaring and Task Management

Once you have figured out how to send, receive, and manage your GroupWise 5 messages, you are ready to get going with the main feature that sets GroupWise 5 apart from most other groupware systems available today — the Calendar.

In Chapter 5, we show you how you can use GroupWise 5 to replace your day planner. We explain how to use the Calendar to manage your Personal Appointments and Tasks, and even how to create Notes to remind you about the events of the day.

Chapter 6: Group Calendaring and Task Management

Once you have mastered the art of maintaining your Personal Notes, Tasks, and Appointments in GroupWise, you are ready begin sending Notes, Tasks, and Appointments to other GroupWise users. We show you how to do this easily in Chapter 6.

In this chapter, we also explain how to use the powerful Busy Search feature to quickly and efficiently access other users' Calendars and find out when people are available for meetings. Finally, we explain how to accept, decline, and delegate Appointments and Tasks you receive in your Mailbox.

Chapter 7: Advanced Features

Chapter 7 delves into some more complex GroupWise 5 features, such as rules, proxies, and discussions (online chat sessions with other GroupWise users).

GroupWise 5 rules are used to automate many of the tasks that you commonly perform in GroupWise 5. For example, you can use rules to automatically reply to certain messages or to automatically move specific messages to a folder.

The Proxy feature enables you to set up GroupWise 5 so that other people can view your Calendar and your messages. You can even give others the power to send messages in your name.

Discussions enable information to be shared across your organization, much like an electronic bulletin board system.

Chapter 8: Document Management

GroupWise Document Management Services (DMS) is cutting-edge technology, tightly integrated with the GroupWise messaging system. Using GroupWise DMS, you can manage your documents through the GroupWise interface and easily share documents with other GroupWise users.

Chapter 8 explains how to import documents into GroupWise libraries, how to create new documents in a library, how to work with documents in a library, and how to share documents with other users.

Chapter 9: Remote Mode

GroupWise 5's Remote Mode enables you to dial in to the main GroupWise 5 system from home or while traveling (assuming that your GroupWise 5 system has been configured to support remote GroupWise access). You can use GroupWise 5 Remote to send messages to others and to receive messages that have been sent to you.

We explain how to use GroupWise Remote to connect to the main GroupWise 5 system through a modem and how to minimize the amount of time you are connected so that you don't run up a huge phone bill. We also explain how to use the Hit the Road feature to keep your Remote Mailbox (on your hard drive) synchronized with your Master Mailbox in the main GroupWise system.

Chapter 10: Customizing GroupWise

To round out the book, we explain how to make GroupWise 5 fit your personal work style by setting GroupWise 5 default options, customizing the Toolbars, and setting folder options. We also give you instructions for setting a password that will prevent someone from hacking into your GroupWise 5 Mailbox.

In addition, the book includes five appendixes. The first three cover GroupWise startup, online help, and Internet features. The fourth appendix features a convenient worksheet for you to record the necessary configuration information to access Remote Mode. In the final appendix, we give an overview of the 16-bit GroupWise client and discuss how it compares with the 32-bit client.

Acknowledgments

I would first like to thank my wife, Kellie, and son, Cameron, for the sacrifices they have made throughout this project.

Thanks also to my co-author and good friend, Rick McTague, for sharing his talents, for his enthusiasm in teaching others about Novell's superior technologies, and for doing more than his fair share with this book. Thanks also to his wonderful family for supporting him in these projects and for their graciousness during my visits to Kansas City.

And finally, on a very personal note, my heartfelt thanks to Jerry Hadlock, Craig Coleman, David Orton, Kim Peterson, Steven Ashby, Lynn Coray, and all of the other wonderful members of the Spanish Fork Mt. Loafer Ward for all they do for me and my family.

Shawn B. Rogers

First of all, I would like to thank my wife, Alison, for all of her support, love, and amazing patience during this project, and also my sons, Richard, Patrick, and James, for understanding why Daddy was in the basement so many nights!

I'd like to thank my mom and dad, my sister Patty, Gavin, my brother Scott and his family, and my parents-in-law, Mom and Dad Turner.

I attribute any success I have had to all of my family. I love you all!

I'd also like to sincerely thank Kevin Grawe, Mitch Morgan, and Steve Harmon of USConnect Kansas City for their continued support, vision, and friendship. I'd also like to thank the whole USConnect gang.

Thanks also to Mike and Lisa Strange, Chris Carspecken, Joe and Fondee Bruce, Rick and Rhonda Stock, and all of our neighbors for all their help and support.

A special thanks goes to Ron Hull at IDG Books, who brought our efforts together and made us readable. Thank you, Ron.

Finally, no acknowledgment would be complete without a tip of the golf cap to my steady and faithful partner, Shawn Rogers. I value tremendously, and do not take for granted, our deep friendship. Thanks to your family, and thanks to you, Shawn.

Rick McTague

We would like to jointly thank Ron Hull at IDG Books for his professionalism and his talents throughout this project. We would also like to thank Bill Mangum for his technical contribution to this book.

We would also like to thank Colleen Bluhm, Rose Kearsley, and Marcy Shanti with Novell Press, and Anne Hamilton and David Kolodney at IDG Books for making this book possible.

Contents at a Glance

Contents

Chapter 5   Personal Calendaring and
Task Management   71

Chapter 6   Group Calendaring and
Task Management   85

CHAPTER 1

Introduction to
GroupWise 5

In this chapter, you will learn about the GroupWise 5 *client interface*. The GroupWise 5 *client* is the software you use to communicate with a main GroupWise 5 system. An *interface* is the end-user's view of a program. It's what you (the user) manipulate to control the program. This chapter briefly introduces you to the main parts of the GroupWise 5 Windows client interface.

There are different versions of GroupWise 5 for the different platforms the program can run on, such as Windows 95, Windows 3.x, Macintosh, and UNIX. Each version has basically the same features, but the way you access those features can vary depending on the capabilities of the environment.

Nevertheless, all GroupWise 5 users deal with common message formats. Because the message format is consistent, each client version can recognize the format of a message and display it in the recipient's native environment, regardless of the version used to create the message. Consequently, you can send messages to people who use different computing platforms without knowing how to use those platforms. For example, you can use the Windows 95 version of GroupWise 5 to schedule meetings with people who use the Windows 3.x and UNIX versions.

Starting GroupWise

To launch GroupWise, double-click on the GroupWise 5 shortcut on your desktop. Normally, GroupWise simply opens up your Mailbox.

The first time you run GroupWise, you may see the *GroupWise Startup screen*. You use this screen to configure your user ID, post office information, and TCP/IP settings. Don't panic if you encounter this screen — your system administrator can give you all the necessary information. We'll assume for the rest of this chapter that you don't need to deal with the Startup screen.

NOTE

Appendix A provides more information about the Startup screen.

The Main GroupWise Screen

When you open the GroupWise 5 client, the screen in Figure 1.1 appears automatically.

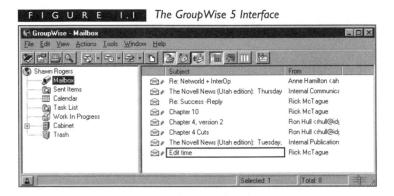

FIGURE 1.1 The GroupWise 5 Interface

You access all GroupWise 5 features from the screen shown in Figure 1.1. We'll call this part of the interface the *main GroupWise screen*. From the main GroupWise screen, you access your incoming messages, outgoing messages, deleted messages, and any items on your Calendar. The GroupWise interface looks very similar to other Windows 95 applications — in particular, it looks a lot like Windows 95 Explorer.

You can open multiple GroupWise windows and customize each one with a different view of your GroupWise information.

TIP

As you can see in Figure 1.1, there are five principal areas of the main screen:

▶ *Menu*. The GroupWise options menu under the title bar.

▶ *Toolbar*. Buttons that provide shortcuts to commonly used menu options.

▶ *Folders List*. The list of the folder icons where your messages are stored.

▶ *Items Area*. The area where messages and other information in a selected folder appear.

▶ *Summary*. An indicator that shows the number of selected items and the total number of messages in the currently selected folder.

The Folders List and Items Area

The two most useful parts of the main GroupWise screen are the Folders List and the Items Area. The Folders List contains a hierarchical structure of folders that are used to organize and hold messages. The Items Area displays the individual messages that are located in the selected folder. The Folders List and Items Area are linked to each other. To view the items in a folder, select the folder in the Folders List on the left; the items in that folder will appear in the Items Area on the right.

There are seven folders that appear automatically in the main GroupWise screen. In Chapter 4, you'll learn how to adjust the settings for these folders and how to create new folders for storing your messages. Table 1.1 lists the seven system-generated, default folders and describes their functions.

TABLE 1.1	*Default Folders*
FOLDER NAME	**DESCRIPTION**
Mailbox	Contains the incoming messages you receive
Sent Items	Stores copies of the messages you have sent
Calendar	Contains your Calendar, which stores information about your Appointments, Notes, and Tasks
Task List	Holds a list of your Tasks
Work In Progress	Keeps drafts of unsent messages until you're ready to send them
Cabinet	Holds all of the messages that you file for storage (It's like your real-world filing cabinet.)
Trash	Contains items you delete

The following subsections describe each of the default system folders in more detail.

Mailbox

When you want to see your new messages, you must open the Mailbox folder. When you receive a new message, an unopened envelope appears next to the Mailbox folder.

Open the Mailbox by single-clicking on it. You will see a list of your opened and unopened messages in the Items Area to the right of the Mailbox, as shown in Figure 1.2.

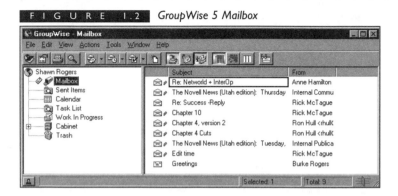

F I G U R E   1.2   *GroupWise 5 Mailbox*

To read a message, simply double-click on the message line. The text portion of the message will appear on the screen.

Sent Items

The Sent Items folder is your "out box." This folder is used to manage messages you have sent. The Sent Items folder enables you to perform three very handy tasks:

- ▶ Viewing the status of messages you have sent
- ▶ Resending messages
- ▶ Retracting messages you have sent (provided they have not been opened yet)

Figure 1.3 shows the Sent Items folder.

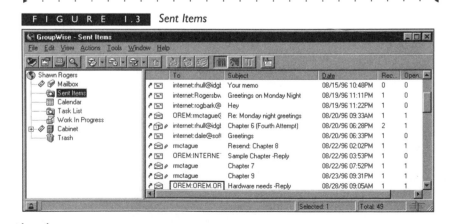

F I G U R E   1.3   *Sent Items*

When you double-click on a sent message, you see complete status information for the message, including when the message was delivered, opened, deleted, completed (if the message was a Task), forwarded, accepted, or declined (if the message was an Appointment).

From Sent Items, you can resend messages that have not been received for some reason. To resend a message, select the Resend option from the Send menu. When you edit and resend a message, you can retract the original message as long as it hasn't been opened yet.

To retract a message, highlight the message in the Sent Items screen and press the Delete key. Next, select Delete from All Mailboxes. This will delete the message from the recipients' Mailboxes, as well as from your own Sent Items folder.

You can only retract e-mail messages that have not been opened.

IMPORTANT

Calendar

The Calendar is where you can create, view, and manage your Appointments, Tasks, and Notes. These Calendar items can be personal items (for example, a Personal Note to yourself), or they can be group items (for example, a Meeting Request). Figure 1.4 shows the Calendar.

Chapters 5 and 6 cover personal and group calendaring in more detail.

NOTE

You can view your Calendar items in the Items Area by clicking on the Calendar folder. To view the Calendar as its own window, click on Window and then choose Calendar. (If you have worked with GroupWise 4, this is the Calendar view you are familiar with.)

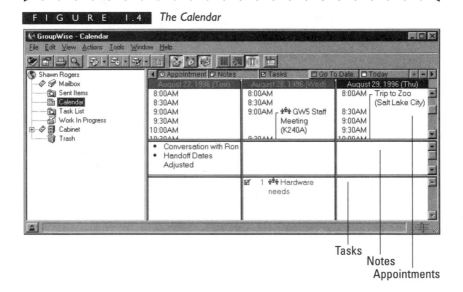

FIGURE 1.4 The Calendar

Tasks
Notes
Appointments

Task List

The Task List displays the Tasks you have created for yourself, as well as those that have been sent to you and you have accepted. Figure 1.5 shows the Task List. (Tasks are explained in more detail in Chapters 5 and 6.)

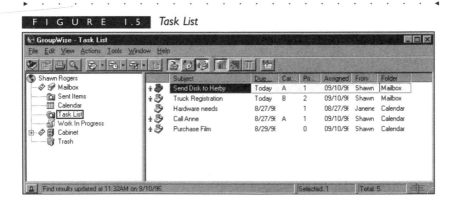

FIGURE 1.5 Task List

A Task is something you need to complete. Each Task has a start date and a due date. Overdue Tasks are carried forward in the Calendar until you mark them complete.

If you send a Task to someone else, and that person accepts it, you can track this Task and find out when it is completed by looking in the Sent Items folder and viewing the Task's status.

Work In Progress

You can use the Work In Progress folder to store drafts of messages that you haven't sent yet, as shown in Figure 1.6.

FIGURE 1.6 *Work In Progress Folder*

If you begin writing a message and you realize you need some information that you don't have yet, save a draft of the message in this folder. When you get the missing information, you can add it to the saved message in the Work In Progress folder and then send the message along.

Cabinet

The Cabinet contains additional folders that you can use to organize your messages. See Figure 1.7 for an example of the Cabinet.

Use the Cabinet folders to organize messages the same way you use the directory and subdirectory structure in the Windows File Manager or Windows Explorer to organize files. You can place messages that pertain to the same project in a folder, nest folders inside other folders, and link messages to multiple folders. (Chapter 4 explains more about folders and how to manage your messages.)

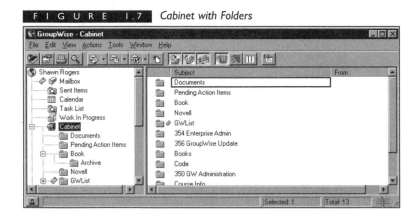

F I G U R E   1.7   *Cabinet with Folders*

Trash

When you delete a message from anywhere in GroupWise 5, the message goes into the Trash. Later, if you need to undelete the message, you can retrieve it from the Trash — provided the Trash has not been emptied. (Chapter 4 discusses managing messages in the Trash folder.)

To view the messages in the Trash, simply click on the Trash folder. Figure 1.8 shows how the Trash folder looks when it's open.

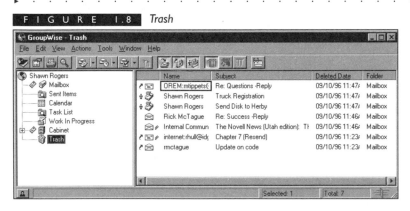

F I G U R E   1.8   *Trash*

Messages do not remain in the Trash forever. They stay there for a certain period of time, and then they are emptied from the Trash. When a message is emptied from the Trash, it is destroyed for good and there is no way to retrieve it. Messages are automatically emptied from the Trash after seven days.

However, you can adjust the number of days that deleted messages stay in the Trash before they are automatically emptied. (Chapter 10 explains how to set this option.)

Navigating through GroupWise

There are many ways to perform individual tasks in GroupWise, and we will try to consistently show you the easiest steps to follow. Like other Windows applications, the GroupWise client contains pull-down menus; scroll bars; and minimize, maximize, and close buttons consistent with Windows 95 conventions. Figure 1.9 shows the GroupWise navigation controls.

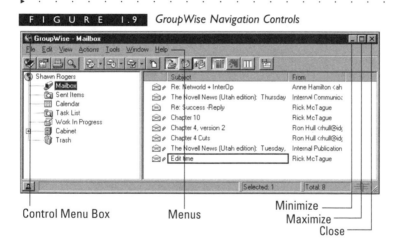

FIGURE 1.9 *GroupWise Navigation Controls*

Control Menu Box   Menus

Minimize
Maximize
Close

You can click on any corner of the interface and drag it to a new position to change the size of the main GroupWise screen. You can also click on and drag the dividing bar between different panes of the main GroupWise screen to resize the panes. Likewise, you can click and drag messages from the Items Area to the Folders List.

Often, you can use alternative methods to execute the menu commands. For example, to send a Mail message, you can click on the File menu, choose New, and Mail Message. Alternatively, you can simply click on the Send Mail button on the Toolbar.

There are several GroupWise features that can help you navigate through GroupWise more quickly. These features are the Toolbar, keystroke shortcuts, QuickMenus, and QuickViewer.

The Toolbar

The Toolbar, shown in Figure 1.10, is the row of buttons under the menu bar in the main GroupWise screen. You can use the buttons on the Toolbar as shortcuts to activate options under the pull-down menus. Using the Toolbar, you can quickly access the GroupWise features you use most often. Editing functions (such as Cut, Copy, and Paste), Spell Check, and Online Help are examples of buttons you can add to the Toolbar, saving you the trouble of selecting these options from the menus. You can use the Toolbar in message views as well as in the main GroupWise screen. (In Chapter 10, we explain how to customize your Toolbar.)

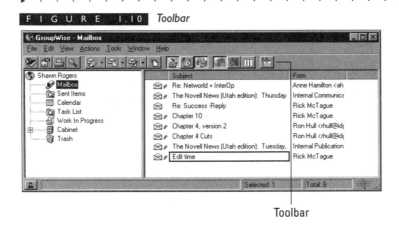

FIGURE 1.10 *Toolbar*

Toolbar

Keystroke Shortcuts

Most menu choices have corresponding keystroke combinations you can use to quickly select them. For example, you can refresh the current folder's message listing by choosing the Refresh option from the View menu, or you can press the F5 key and get the same result.

QuickMenus

QuickMenus, shown in Figure 1.11, are a feature of GroupWise 5 that add functionality to the right mouse button. When you are accessing different areas of the interface, a right-click of the mouse displays a short menu of actions.

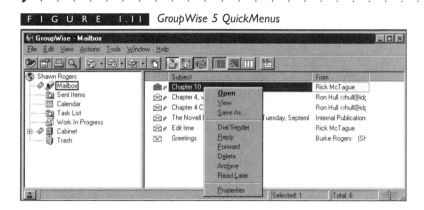

FIGURE 1.11   *GroupWise 5 QuickMenus*

QuickViewer

By enabling the GroupWise QuickViewer, you can read messages without double-clicking on them. A third, lower window pane displays the contents of messages that have been selected, as shown in Figure 1.12. When you select a message in the Items Area, the QuickViewer pane of the main GroupWise screen displays the message contents automatically.

FIGURE 1.12   *QuickViewer Enabled*

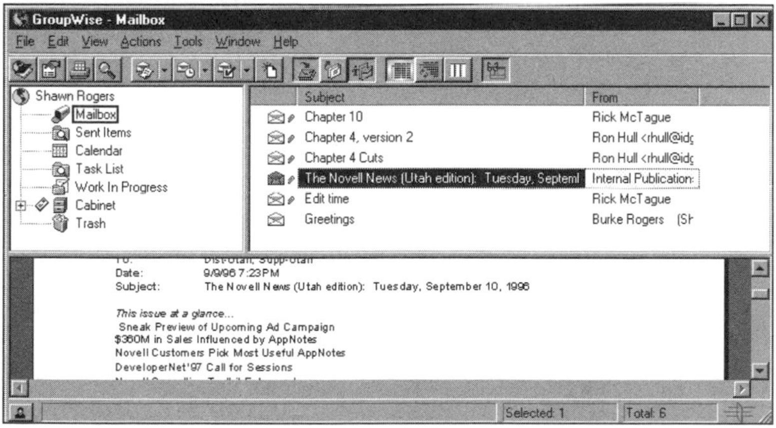

Summary

In this chapter, you learned about the GroupWise 5 interface, which gives you access to many different messaging and calendaring functions. You also learned some tricks that will help you navigate through the interface. The next chapter covers the messaging features of GroupWise 5 in greater detail.

CHAPTER 2

Messaging
Fundamentals

This chapter teaches you the fundamentals of GroupWise messaging. GroupWise is more than just an e-mail program: GroupWise is a personal time manager, a group scheduler, and an e-mail program all rolled into one. As you saw in Chapter 1, there are several types of GroupWise messages. Typically, there are Mail messages, Phone messages, Appointments, Tasks, and Notes; other types of messages are available in enhanced GroupWise systems. You can send all of these message types to other users. You can also use GroupWise messages to keep track of your own schedule. Keep in mind that proper use of *all* message types is essential if you want to use GroupWise most effectively.

GroupWise 5 uses icons to represent different message types and to reflect changes in the status of messages. By glancing at any icon in your Mailbox, you can identify which type of message it represents. You can also tell whether the message has file attachments, what its priority level is, and whether you have already opened the message.

Figure 2.1 shows how different message icons appear in the GroupWise Mailbox when the corresponding messages are either opened or unopened. You should familiarize yourself with the different message icons so you can easily manage the different message types.

F I G U R E   2 . 1   *GroupWise Message Icons*

Other visual cues give different kinds of information about messages in the Mailbox. A paper clip next to a message indicates that the message includes a file attachment (or multiple attachments). A loudspeaker icon means that a sound file is attached. A red message icon indicates a high-priority message, and a gray message icon indicates a low-priority message. (We explain how to set message priorities in Chapter 10.)

Message Types

When you're talking about GroupWise, the word "message" has many different meanings. You can send and receive five basic message types with GroupWise 5: Mail messages, Appointments, Tasks, Notes, and Phone messages. (Additional message types are available if you have an enhanced system, such as Voice Mail messages and Fax messages. Check with your system administrator if you are not sure whether your system has enhanced capabilities.)

Mail Messages

A *Mail message* (also called an *e-mail message*) is like a memo. It has one or more recipients, a subject line, and a date. In addition, Mail messages contain fields where you can specify recipients of carbon copies and blind copies. We focus on Mail messages in this chapter.

To create a Mail message, click on the Create New Mail icon on the Toolbar, or click on File, New, and then Mail.

Appointments

You can create two types of Appointments: Personal Appointments and Meetings. Your Personal Appointments are entries you make in your own Calendar to keep track of your personal engagements. Meetings are group Appointments that you can use to schedule meetings with other GroupWise users.

When another user sends you a request for a Meeting and you accept it, the Meeting automatically moves to your Calendar. If you decline a Meeting request, the message status information in the sender's Mailbox tells the sender that you have declined the Meeting.

TIP

Instead of using standard e-mail messages to schedule meetings, create GroupWise Meetings. Standard e-mail messages do not automatically create entries in recipients' Calendars. When you use standard e-mail messages for scheduling, recipients must take the time to mark their Calendars with Personal Appointments.

To create a Personal Appointment, click on the down arrow button next to the Appointment icon on the Toolbar, and then click Personal Appointment.

To create a Meeting, from the File menu click on New and then on Appointment. Alternatively, click on the Create New Appointment button on the Toolbar.

Tasks

You can use a Task message to delegate or assign tasks to other GroupWise users. You can also create Personal Tasks for your personal Task List.

TIP Instead of using e-mail messages to delegate assignments, send a Task. Tasks automatically appear in the recipients' Task Lists, and you can conveniently specify a priority and a due date for each Task.

When someone receives and accepts a Task, the Task appears in the recipient's Task List folder and in the Task section of the recipient's Calendar view. The Task is carried forward each day until that person marks it as "Completed." If the recipient does not mark a Task as completed by the specified due date, the Task turns red in both the Task List and in the Calendar view.

To create a Personal Task, click on the down arrow next to the Create New Task button on the Toolbar, and then choose Personal Task.

Notes

You can use Notes to create notes for yourself or to send reminders to other GroupWise users. When someone receives and accepts a Note, the Note automatically moves to the Notes: field in the recipient's Calendar view. Unlike a Task, however, a Note is not carried over from day to day. You enter Notes into the Calendar only on the date specified.

TIP If you want to create a Note that appears regularly — for example, to remind yourself when it's payday — you can use the Auto-Date feature, further explained in Chapter 6.

To create a Personal Note, open your Calendar view and double-click inside the Notes: field. To send someone else a Note, click on File, New, and then Note.

Send Notes to members of your workgroup notifying them of days and times when you will be away from your desk, in meetings, or on vacation. This action will remind the people in your workgroup where you are on the specified days.

Phone Messages

Use Phone messages to inform other GroupWise users about phone calls you have taken for them. A Phone message is very similar to an e-mail message. The Phone message window includes fields for caller information (such as name, company, and phone number) and a description of the call ("Urgent," "Please call," "Returned your call," and so forth). Phone messages are basically electronic versions of preprinted message forms.

To create a Phone message or While You Were Out message, click on File, New, and then Phone message.

Because Phone messages are so similar to regular e-mail messages, with the exception of the fields in the view, we will not discuss Phone messages further.

Alternate E-Mail Views

Views are display formats for GroupWise messages and interface components. For example, a Mail message has three views associated with it: Mail, Expanded Mail, and Small Mail. You can choose a view that excludes the features you don't need or one that has a larger-than-normal message area.

NOTE

Alternate views do not prevent you from using all of the GroupWise features. In alternate views, you may not see certain shortcut methods for activating features, but you can always use the pull-down menus to access those features.

Small Mail

The Small Mail view provides a concise message area without the file attachment, CC:, or BC: buttons, as shown in Figure 2.2. Use this view when you need to send a short message to someone.

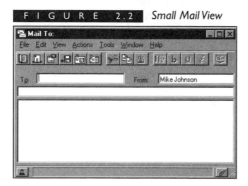

F I G U R E   2 . 2   *Small Mail View*

To send an e-mail message using the Small Mail view, choose New from the File menu, and then select Mail. From the message's pull-down menus, choose Edit, Change To, and then More. Highlight the Mail (Small) option and click on OK.

Expanded Mail

The Expanded Mail view enables more screen "real estate" to be used for the message portion of your e-mail. This view displays more of the message on screen, which is handy for people who don't like to scroll down through long messages. To send an e-mail using the Expanded Mail view, choose New from the File menu and select Mail. Then, from the message pull-down menu, choose Edit, Change To, More, click on the Expanded Mail option, and then click on OK. Figure 2.3 shows the Expanded Mail view. (You can set the Expanded or Small Mail view as your default message view, as explained in Chapter 10.)

FIGURE 2.3 *Expanded Mail View*

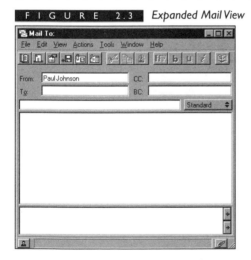

Sending GroupWise Messages

The GroupWise dialog box for sending messages is very easy to use. The message dialog box is essentially a form you complete for each message you send. While the different message types may have different fields to fill in, several fields are common to all message types. In this section we focus on sending e-mail messages, but the concepts are basically the same for all GroupWise message types.

To send a message, you must enter someone's e-mail address (such as msmith@acme.com) or enter the GroupWise user name in the To: field. You can also use the Address Book to enter user addresses. (Chapter 3 covers the Address Book in depth.)

The Send Mail dialog box appears in Figure 2.4.

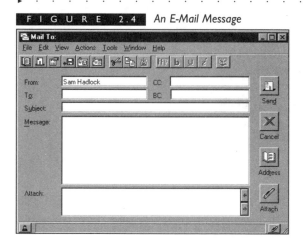

F I G U R E   2 . 4   *An E-Mail Message*

To send an e-mail message:

1. Click on File, New, and then Mail. Alternatively, you can click on the Create New Mail button on the Toolbar.

2. Select the recipients using the Address Book or by typing their names in the To:, CC:, and BC: fields. Separate multiple user names with commas. (Address Book techniques are explained in Chapter 3.)

3. Add a subject line in the Subject: field.

4. Type your message in the Message: field.

5. Click on the Send button to send the message.

The recipients listed in the To: field are the primary recipients of the message. Primary recipients can view the message information screen and see all other primary recipients and all CC: (carbon copy) recipients, but they cannot see the names of BC: (blind copy) recipients. The people listed in the CC: field receive a copy of the message. Carbon copy recipients can also see all of the primary recipients and other carbon copy recipients, but they cannot see blind copy recipients. People who receive a blind copy can see all primary recipients and all carbon copy recipients, but they cannot see other blind copy recipients.

If you want to send a message to multiple people, but you don't want any of them to know who else received the message, make them all blind copy recipients. For example, you could use this technique to inform job applicants that a position has been filled if you don't want the applicants to know who else applied for the job. Because you must include at least one primary recipient, insert your own name in the To: field.

Saving Draft Messages in the Work In Progress Folder

As you compose a message, you may find a need to save your work and resume your message later. You can save messages you are working on in the Work In Progress folder.

To save a message in the Work In Progress folder:

1. With the message open, choose Save Draft from the File menu.

2. Select the Work In Progress folder and click on OK.

To resume working on a draft message:

1. Open the Work In Progress folder.

2. Double-click on the message you want to finish.

3. Finish the message and choose Send.

A message can be saved as a draft message at any point during its composition. You can also attach files to a message; they will be saved along with the message in the Work In Progress folder.

WiseGuide

Here's an alternative way to save a message in Work In Progress:

1. When you decide you need to work on a message later, click on Cancel with the message open. You are prompted to save the message.

2. Choose Yes, and save the message to the Work in Progress folder.

If you modify a file that is attached to a message in the Work In Progress folder, be sure you delete the file attachment icon and reattach the message. Otherwise, the original version of the file will be sent.

Attaching Files to a Message

You can share documents, spreadsheets, database files, or other files by sending them to other users as file attachments to a GroupWise message. You can attach files to any GroupWise message, even if the message type does not include a file attachment field in the dialog box.

To attach a file to an e-mail message:

1. In the e-mail dialog box, click on the Attach button.

2. Choose Select File to attach a file, or choose Insert Object to attach an OLE object, such as a .WAV sound file.

3. Browse to the location of the file, select the desired file, click on Open to place the file in the attachments list, and select Close to attach the file to the message

An icon representing the attachment appears at the bottom of the e-mail window. The attached file or object will travel along with your message to the recipient. Figure 2.5 shows an e-mail message with an attachment.

F I G U R E 2.5 *Message with an Attachment*

Some GroupWise message types, such as Appointments and Tasks, do not include an Attach: window in the message form. However, you can still attach files to these message types by clicking on File and then Attachments. When you attach a file to a message type that does not include an Attach: window, make a note in the message text that you have attached a file. Otherwise, the recipients will not know there is a file attached when they receive the message.

NOTE

Click on the paper clip icon at the bottom of message windows to open the Attachments dialog box.

Attaching an OLE Object

You can attach an Object Linking and Embedding (OLE) object to a GroupWise message. When you have an OLE object (a chart, for instance) linked to some other data (such as a spreadsheet), the OLE object is updated whenever changes are made to the linked data.

To attach an OLE object to a GroupWise message:

1. From the e-mail message, choose OLE from the Edit menu, and select Attach Object.

2. Select the object from its source.

3. Choose Attach New Object and select the appropriate source object (a Microsoft Word document, for example), and then select Attach New.

Figure 2.6 shows an attached OLE object.

Reading Messages

The messages you receive are initially stored in your Mailbox folder (also called simply "the Mailbox").

To read a message:

1. Click on the Mailbox to display a list of the messages you have received in the Items Area.

2. Double-click on the desired message, or highlight the message and press Enter.

The message opens for you to read.

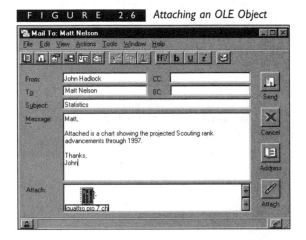

F I G U R E   2 . 6   *Attaching an OLE Object*

TIP

Use the QuickViewer to quickly read several messages in succession. To activate the QuickViewer, click on View and then on QuickViewer. A third pane will open at the bottom of the GroupWise window and will display the contents of the message that you have highlighted.

Viewing File Attachments

When you receive a message with a file attachment, you can use the built-in viewers in GroupWise to view the file's contents. From a viewer screen, you can launch the associated application or save the attachment. Figure 2.7 shows a file attachment opened by a viewer.

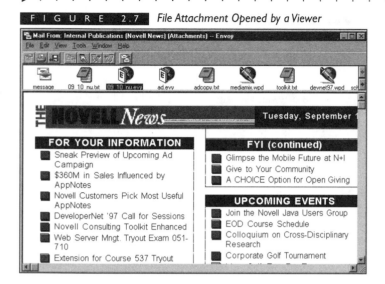

F I G U R E   2.7   *File Attachment Opened by a Viewer*

The first time you view a file attachment, GroupWise generates the viewers for all supported file formats. GroupWise only generates the viewers the first time you view an attachment after GroupWise is installed (or if you have installed updated viewer files), and it usually takes less than a minute to generate them.

The first time you receive a Mail message with an attachment and double-click on the attachment icon, you will be prompted to indicate what function you want double-clicking to launch. You can choose to have attachments open in a viewer (choose *View* as the default action) or in the associated applications (choose *Open* as the default action). If you change your mind later, you can adjust this setting using the Options feature under the Tools menu.

To view a file attachment from an open message, double-click on the attachment icon (if you selected View as the default action) or right-click on the attachment icon and select View Attachment.

To launch an application associated with the attached file, double-click on the attachment icon (if you selected Open as the default action) or right-click on the attachment icon and select Open.

Replying to Messages

GroupWise enables you to have electronic conversations and maintain a record of what each person says. When you respond to another person's message, you can reply to the sender only or reply to all recipients of the message. You can also include the original message in your reply. When you include a copy of the original message, you can insert your comments at the top of the message or at various points throughout the message. Figure 2.8 shows your message reply options.

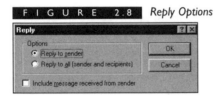

F I G U R E 2.8 *Reply Options*

To reply to a message:

1. While the message is open, click on Reply.

2. Choose either Reply to Sender or Reply to All.

3. *Optional.* Select Include Message Received from Sender if you want to include a copy of the original message in your response.

TIP Use the Reply to All option judiciously. Make sure that everyone who received the original message really needs to see your reply.

The sender's name (and all recipients' names if you selected Reply to All) automatically appears in the To: field. The Subject: field of the original message is retained, with the abbreviation "Re:" in front of it. If you selected Include Message Received from Sender, the original message text appears in the reply message. When you type your reply, it appears above the original message unless you move the cursor to another location. Figure 2.9 shows a reply that appears above the original message.

A Reply that Includes the Original Message

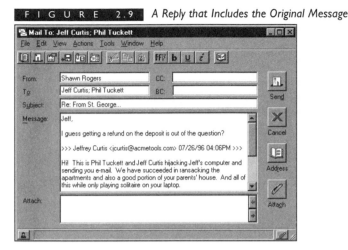

Reply messages do not automatically include the file attachments from the original message. However, you can attach files to a reply message.

Forwarding Messages

If you want to pass along a message or its file attachment to someone else, you should *forward* the message. When you forward a message, you send a new message with the old message as an attachment. The original message remains intact along with its file attachments, as shown in Figure 2.10. It is a good idea to always include your own introductory message when you forward a message.

To forward a message:

1. While the message to be forwarded is open, click on the Forward button or choose Forward from the Actions menu. A new message screen opens. The original message appears as an attachment with the message subject as the name of the attachment.

2. Use the Address Book (or enter the user names) to fill in the To: field and type a message to the recipient(s).

3. Click on Send to forward the message.

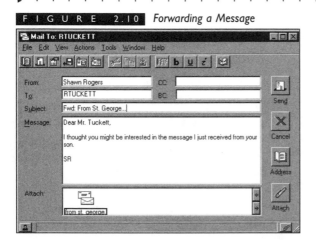

Forwarding a Message

When you forward a message, you actually create a new message, which contains a copy of the original message and its file attachments. A copy of the original message remains in your Mailbox. You can delete the original message if you don't need it, or store it in a folder.

When a recipient opens the forwarded message, he or she accesses the original message and its file attachments by double-clicking on the Mail message icon in the Attach: field.

Deleting Messages

When you no longer need a message, you can delete it from your Mailbox. After you delete it, the message goes to the Trash folder. The message remains there until you empty the Trash manually or until the Trash is emptied automatically, according to what you set up in GroupWise Options.

To delete a message, select the message and press the Delete key. Or, click on the message and drag it to the Trash folder.

You can delete messages from any location (for example, from the Mailbox folder, the Sent Items folder, or from any Calendar view).

Restoring Messages

When you delete a message, it goes to the Trash folder and stays there until you empty the Trash. While the message is stored in the Trash, you can "undelete" or restore the message to its original location.

To restore a message to the location it was deleted from:

1. Open the Trash folder.

2. Highlight the message.

3. Choose Undelete from the Edit menu.

Alternatively, you can right-click on the message and choose Undelete from the QuickMenu. The message will be restored to its previous location.

Summary

In this chapter, you learned the fundamentals of GroupWise messaging. We explained how to send and read messages, how to send replies, how to forward messages, and how to delete messages you no longer need. Chapter 3 explains how to use the GroupWise Address Book to improve your productivity with GroupWise even more.

CHAPTER 3

Using the GroupWise Address Book

The GroupWise Address Book is your GroupWise yellow pages; it's your master directory for looking up information about other users. Just as a telephone book lists more than just telephone numbers, the Address Book lists more than just GroupWise user IDs. You can find other users' phone numbers, fax numbers, departments, and much more.

Use the Address Book to:

▸ Find GroupWise user IDs when addressing GroupWise messages

▸ Send messages to groups of users; for example, to all members of a specific department

▸ Create personal groups that list the users you often send messages to

▸ Look up information about other GroupWise users

▸ Create personal address books that contain addresses of users within and outside of the GroupWise system, such as people you commonly correspond with on the Internet

▸ Create address profiles, such as all users who have the job title Director or all users who work in a specific building

▸ Dial your telephone (if GroupWise Conversation Place is enabled)

NOTE *GroupWise Conversation Place* is a telephone integration program that links GroupWise with your telephone system. If you don't know whether you can use Conversation Place, ask your system administrator.

Address Book Features

The main components of the Address Book are:

▸ Search fields

▸ Menus

▸ System and personal address books

▸ To:, BC:, and CC: fields

▸ Information field headings

Figure 3.1 shows the GroupWise Address Book with its main components labeled.

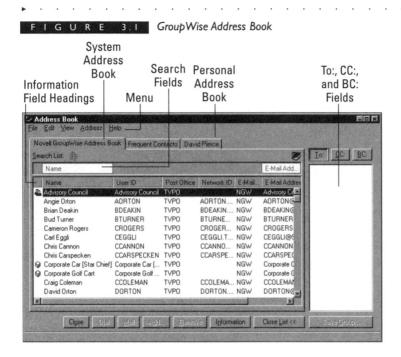

F I G U R E 3.1 *GroupWise Address Book*

System Address Book — Search Fields — Personal Address Book — To:, CC:, and BC: Fields — Information Field Headings — Menu

NOTE

When we refer to the "Address Book" (capitalized) we mean the Address Book program that is part of GroupWise. When we refer to "address book" (lower case) we are referring to one of the individual directories — such as the system address book or the Frequent Contacts address book — that contain lists of users.

WiseGuide

You can access the Address Book to address a GroupWise message by simply clicking on the Address Book icon in the message view.

You can access the Address Book in a number of ways. For instance, you can run the Address Book as a stand-alone program outside of GroupWise. Used in this way, the Address Book is a very handy company directory. If you create an Address Book icon in Windows 95, you can quickly access the Address Book to look up phone numbers, addresses, and other information.

To set up an icon for the Address Book in Windows 95:

1. Use Explorer or the My Computer icon to locate ADDRBOOK.EXE. (It is typically located in the NOVELL\GROUPWISE directory.)

2. Right-click on the ADDRBOOK.EXE file and drag it to your desired location.

3. Choose the Create Shortcut Here option from the pop-up menu.

You can also use the Address Book to address GroupWise messages to people. To launch the Address Book from within GroupWise, choose Address Book from the Tools menu (or click on the Address Book icon on the Toolbar).

Notice in Figure 3.1 that the Address Book has three tabs — one labeled Novell GroupWise Address Book, one labeled Frequent Contacts, and one with a GroupWise user name.

The *Novell GroupWise address book* (the system address book) is the master address book for your GroupWise system. All users in the system are visible in this address book.

The *Frequent Contacts address book* lists the users that you have recently sent messages to or received messages from. These users are listed in alphabetical order. The Frequent Contacts address book enables you to quickly send messages to the people you correspond with most often.

The address book tab with your name on it is a personal address book that you use to add names, e-mail addresses, and other personal information about users you correspond with. The users listed in the personal address book do not have to be GroupWise users (or even e-mail users, for that matter). You can use a personal address book to store all of your contact information. Later in this chapter, we'll explain how to create additional personal address books.

To switch between the various address books, simply click on the appropriate tab.

To close an address book that you don't want to use, click on the address book tab, then choose Close Book from the File menu.

You can change the way information is displayed in the Address Book by moving or modifying the headings. To move a heading from one location to another, simply click on and drag the heading to a new location. To remove a heading, click and drag it from the headings bar. To replace a heading that has been deleted, right-click on an empty area of the headings bar and select the

WiseGuide

You can determine the sort order for personal address books by right-clicking on the tab and choosing either Ascending or Descending.

heading you want to add. You can resize headings by clicking on and dragging the line that separates two headings.

Addressing Messages with the Address Book

When sending a message to more than one person, it is usually much easier to address GroupWise messages with the Address Book than it is to type in user names. Also, you don't need to worry about misspelling user names when you use the Address Book.

Use the arrow keys or the scroll bar to locate an addressee, and then double-click on the user's name to insert that name in the To: field of the Address Book. Insert any additional names, and then choose OK to return to your message. The recipients will be inserted in the To: field of the message.

The user list is searchable. To find an addressee, begin typing the person's name. If your address book is sorted by last name, begin typing the user's last name. If the list is sorted by first name, begin typing the user's first name. (We'll talk more about different searching techniques later in this chapter.)

The right column (where the users are listed when you select them from the Address Book) defaults to the To: field. GroupWise assumes that most of the users you send the message to are the primary recipients and should be added to the message's To: field. Consequently, when you select users from the address list, they are listed in the To: field by default. To add BC: or CC: recipients, click on the corresponding button before adding users.

If you have a user in the To: field that needs to be moved to either the CC: or BC: field, right-click on the user and choose the appropriate field from the QuickMenu.

> **WiseGuide**
>
> Use the Address Book to get information about other users, such as their fax numbers or employee IDs, by highlighting the user in the user list and clicking the Info button.

Sending Messages to Groups

A GroupWise group is a list of users that you can send messages to. There are two types of address book groups: public groups and personal groups.

A *public group* is a list of users defined by the system administrator for convenient message addressing. All GroupWise users have access to the system's public groups, unless they have been excluded by the system administrator.

For example, your system administrator may create a distribution list called Sales that includes all members of the sales organization. Public groups are located in the system address book.

A *personal group* is a list of users you create to automate your messaging. For example, you can create personal groups that include the members of each project you work on. (Personal groups only display in personal address books. They do not display in the system address book.)

Groups are listed in the Address Book along with individual users. They are distinguished from users by a *group icon,* as shown in Figure 3.2.

FIGURE 3.2 *Groups in the Address Book*

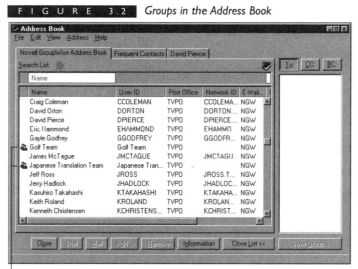

Groups

Addressing Messages to Groups

To address a message to a group:

1. Click on the Address icon from within a message view.

2. Double-click on the group to add the group name to the To: field, or select the group and click on the To:, CC:, or BC: button to add the group name to the appropriate address field.

3. Click on OK.

(If you know the name of the group, you don't have to use the Address Book. Just type the group name in your message's To: field.)

To search for groups, simply begin typing the name of the group. When GroupWise finds the group you want, you can stop typing.

NOTE If you want to send a message to most, but not all, members of a group, right-click on the group and choose the Edit Group option. The members of the group will be listed individually in the To: field. You can then delete individual group members from the To: field.

Creating Personal Groups

You can create personal groups that appear in your personal address book. To create a personal group:

1. Open an address book (for example, the system address book) that contains the users you want to include in a personal group.

2. Add the users you want in the group to the To:, CC:, and BC: fields in the same manner you would use when addressing a message.

3. Click on the Save Group button.

4. Name the group, specify which personal address book the group should be added to, and then click on OK.

You can include users from different address books in one group.

Creating Personal Address Books

Personal address books are address books you create that list users you often correspond with. Personal address books can contain users who are in the GroupWise system or users who are external to the GroupWise system, such as Internet users. (Remember, the Novell GroupWise address book is the system address book and only the administrator can add to or modify the listings in this address book.)

NOTE Personal *groups* are customized groupings of users that you can address messages to by typing the group name in the To: field. Personal *address books* are like personal Rolodexes. In personal address books, you can store information about users, organizations, or resources.

You can create an unlimited number of personal address books within the Address Book to organize your contacts. For example, you can create separate personal address books for key contacts in other companies, for your friends and family, and for people you correspond with over the Internet.

By default, GroupWise creates one personal address book for you. Your personal address book has your name on the address book tab.

To create a new personal address book:

1. With the Address Book open, click on File, and then on New Book.

2. Name the new address book and choose OK. The address book tab will appear in the main Address Book window.

3. Click on the Add button.

4. Choose Person, Resource, or Organization.

5. Fill in the fields for the entry.

6. Click on OK.

Keep in mind the following points about personal address books:

▸ You can create, edit, and save any number of personal address books.

▸ You can add and delete names and address information for any person, resource, or company in your personal address books, but *you cannot modify information in your system address book.*

▸ The same name can be included in multiple address books. If you copy an entry from one address book to another and then later modify the entry, it will be updated in all address books that contain the entry.

▸ Internet addresses can be included in personal address books.

▸ You do not have to display all address books in the Address Book main window. To choose which books you want open, use the Open Book and Close Book options in the File menu to specify which address books appear.

▸ You can define custom fields for your personal address books. See the topic, "Create My Own Fields and Columns" in the Address Book online help system for instructions.

TIP To send a message to everyone in a personal address book, click the address book tab to make the address book active, choose Edit, Select All, and then click on the To: button.

To edit an entry in a personal address book, highlight the entry, and choose Edit from the Edit menu.

To delete a personal address book:

1. Click on File.

2. Click on Delete Book.

3. Highlight the book or books you want to delete.

4. Click on OK.

5. Click on Yes to confirm the deletion.

Searching the Address Book

You can search for Address Book information by using the Search List box, by using a predefined address filter, or by defining your own filter.

The Search List Box

To search for an address using the Search List box:

1. Click on the tab of the address book you want to search.

2. In the Search List box, begin typing what you are searching for. GroupWise will place information that matches your search criteria in the search box.

3. When GroupWise finds the information you are searching for, click on the To: field to insert the address.

Figure 3.3 shows the Search List box.

F I G U R E   3.3 *Address Book Search Fields*

Search Fields

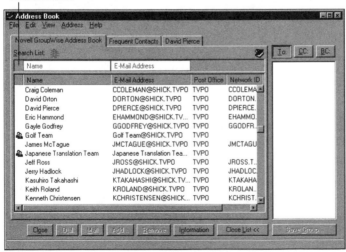

Predefined Address Filters

In GroupWise, a *filter* refers to a set of conditions that remove selected items from a list. For example, you can use a message filter to stop unopened messages from appearing in your Mailbox or an address book filter to display only resources or groups. You'll learn more about using filters in Chapter 4.

By default, address books display *all* entries that have been incorporated into them. Consequently, in large address books, individuals and groups can be difficult to locate. By using a *predefined filter*, you can display only the information you are looking for.

The Address Book has four predefined filters: Filter for Groups, Filter for People, Filter for Organizations, and Filter for Resources. In addition, you can define your own customized address filters.

To use a predefined filter while using the Address Book:

1. Click on View.

2. Click on Predefined Filters.

3. Click on the filter you want to use.

After you enable filtering, a check mark appears next to the Filtering Enabled option on the View menu and a filter icon appears at the upper left of an address book tab. Only the users, groups, organizations, or resources specified in the filter appear in the address list.

Figure 3.4 shows the GroupWise Address Book filtered to show only resources. Notice that the filter icon appears next to "Search List."

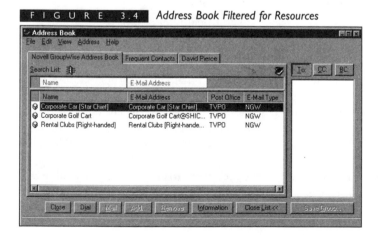

FIGURE 3.4 *Address Book Filtered for Resources*

To return to the regular (nonfiltered) Address Book view, click on View and then on the Filtering Enabled check box to remove the check mark and disable filtering.

User-Defined Filters

You can design customized filters to help you with common address book searches. For example, if you often send a message to all managers in a company, you might define a filter that searches for all managers. By using this filter to send a message to managers, you ensure that the message is sent to people with that title.

Using customized filters is often more efficient than creating personal groups because groups quickly become outdated. A filter ensures that only current users in the address book receive your message.

To create a filter:

1. Click on View.

2. Click on Define Filter. The Filter dialog box appears. The first column lists the columns available in the address book.

3. Click on a column.

4. Click on the Operator drop-down box to select an operator.

5. Type a parameter in the Parameter text box. By default, the Parameter drop-down box displays End.

6. If you want to choose additional parameters, click the Parameter drop-down box and choose an operator.

7. Repeat steps 3–6 to establish additional filter criteria.

8. When you have defined the filter, choose End in the final parameter's drop-down box, and then click on OK.

An *operator* is a symbol that represents a mathematical operation. A *parameter* is a variable used with a command to indicate a specific value or option. For example, to create a filter that lists only users with the last name Williams, click on the Last Name column, click on the = button (the equal sign button), and then type Williams. In this example, = is the operator and Williams is the parameter.

Here is another example. Suppose you want to create a filter that addresses a message to all managers in the sales department of your company. Follow these steps:

1. Click on View.

2. Select Define Filter.

3. Click on the Column drop-down list and select Department.

4. Click on the Operator box and choose =.

5. Enter the name of the department (for example, Sales) in the Parameter box.

6. Click on the Parameter drop-down box and choose And.

7. Click on the Column drop-down list and select Title.

8. Click on the Operator box and choose =.

9. Enter Manager in the Parameter box.

10. Choose End from the Parameter drop-down list.

11. Choose OK to apply the filter.

Figure 3.5 shows the filter dialog box for the previous example.

FIGURE 3.5 *Sales Manager Filter*

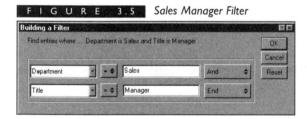

Sharing Personal Address Books

You can use the Address Book's export and import features to share personal address books with other users.

Suppose that you are an administrative assistant who maintains a personal address book for the entire department. The department address book would be very useful to share with other users. Simply export the file and send it to other users, who then import the file and use it in one of their own personal address books.

To export an address book:

1. Open the address book you wish to export.

2. Click on File and then on Export.

3. Choose Entire Address Book or Selected Items.

4. Name the address book file. (Address book export files have a .NAB file extension.)

5. Choose Save.

You can now send this file to other users as an attachment to a message. They can then import the file.

To import a personal address book file:

1. Highlight the personal address book to which the group will be imported, or create a new personal address book to contain the imported users.

2. Click on File and then on Import.

3. Locate the .NAB file and choose Open.

NOTE

You cannot import users into your system address book.

Using the Address Book to Call Other Users

If GroupWise Conversation Place has been enabled on your system, you can use the Address Book to automatically dial other users on the telephone. To dial a phone number from the Address Book:

1. Locate the person you wish to dial in an address book.

2. Click on Dial. If an address entry contains only one phone number, the Address Book dials that number. If there is more than one number, you are prompted for which number you want to use.

3. If prompted for the phone number, choose a phone number from the Available Numbers dialog box and click on OK.

Summary

In this chapter we explained how to use the GroupWise Address Book to automate mail message addressing and to organize information about people you frequently correspond with. In Chapter 4, we'll explain how to efficiently manage your messages to prevent information overload.

CHAPTER 4

Message
Management

As messaging technology advances, more and more message types are being created. In a standard GroupWise system, the Mailbox displays Mail messages, Phone messages, Appointments, Tasks, Notes, and Documents.

With GroupWise add-on products, the Mailbox can also display other kinds of messages, such as Fax messages and Voice Mail messages. With all of these different message types available, you need some way to manage your messages, to prevent information overload and to eliminate clutter from your GroupWise Mailbox. This chapter explains how to use different GroupWise features to organize and manage your messages.

► · ◄

Archiving Messages

The primary method for storing messages indefinitely is called *archiving*. An archived message is not stored in your Mailbox (which is on a GroupWise server); rather it is stored on your local hard drive or in your user directory on the network. Archiving messages gives you access to your old messages without cluttering up your active Mailbox. You can archive messages that have been sent to you as well as messages you have sent to others. The process of archiving messages is fairly easy. In fact, you can set up the GroupWise 5 client so archiving happens automatically when messages have been sitting in your Mailbox for a certain period of time.

You cannot archive messages when using GroupWise Remote.

NOTE

Before you can archive messages, you must specify a location where your archived messages will be stored. This location is usually on your hard drive. If you have questions about the location of your archive directory, ask your system administrator.

To specify an archive directory:

1. Click on Tools and select Options.

2. Double-click on the Environment icon and choose the File Location tab, as shown in Figure 4.1.

3. Enter a directory path in the Archive directory field, or browse to a directory on your hard drive.

4. Click on OK and then on Close.

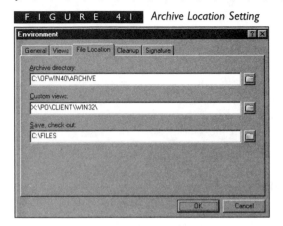

To archive messages:

1. From a folder (for example, the Mailbox or the Sent Items folder), select a message or group of messages. (You can select a range of messages by pressing Shift and clicking on the beginning and end of the range. You can select multiple, nonadjacent messages by pressing Ctrl and clicking on the messages.)

2. Choose Actions.

3. Choose Archive.

The selected messages move to your local archive storage file.

To have GroupWise automatically archive messages after a certain length of time, choose Tools, Options, Environment, and then Cleanup. (See Chapter 10 for customizing these options.) You can adjust the period of time that Mail messages, Phone messages, Appointments, Tasks, and Notes remain in your Mailbox before they are automatically archived. Automatic archiving will then take place as needed each time you exit GroupWise.

Viewing Archived Messages

To view an archived message:

1. Select File, and then choose Open Archive. The messages stored in the *Archive Mailbox* are listed. As Figure 4.2 illustrates, "(Archive)" appears on the title bar to indicate that you are looking at archived messages. If you view the File menu again, you see that a check mark appears next to the Open Archive option. The check mark indicates that the archive is currently open.

2. Double-click on the message you want to read. If you are using the QuickViewer (see Chapter 1), the contents of the archived message appear in the bottom message pane.

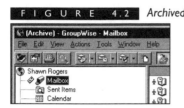

FIGURE 4.2 *Archived Messages*

To return to your Mailbox from an archive, click on File and then deselect Open Archive. The active folder and its contents appear. If you look at the File menu again, you see there is no longer a check mark next to the Open Archive option. The check mark disappears when the regular Mailbox is active, and "(Archive)" disappears from the title bar.

Unarchiving Messages

To *unarchive* a message or group of messages:

1. With your Archive Mailbox open, select the message or group of messages you want to move back to your active Mailbox.

2. Click on Actions and then deselect Archive. (The Archive option is a toggle switch. When a message is archived, a check mark appears next to the Archive option in the File menu.)

The selected messages will be removed from your hard drive on a GroupWise server. You should now be able to see the messages in your regular Mailbox or Sent Items folder.

Saving Messages

Saving messages is different from archiving. When you save a message, you transfer the message information into a separate file. This file can then be used in a word processing program or other application. When you archive a message, the message is not deleted from your Mailbox; GroupWise merely saves a copy of it in a separate file.

To save a message:

1. From the In Box, select the message and then choose Save under the File menu.

2. As Figure 4.3 shows, highlight the message, specify the destination directory and filename for the message, and click on Save to save the message as a file. The message is saved as a WordPerfect-compatible document. A default filename is created from the Subject: field (you can create your own filename) and the extension .MLM is added to the end of the filename.

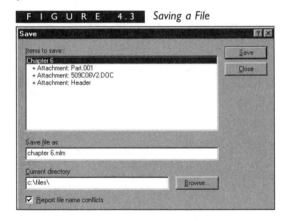

FIGURE 4.3 *Saving a File*

Printing Messages

The Print option under the File menu enables you to specify custom print settings. To select paper type, fonts, and other options:

1. Click on the File menu.

2. Choose Print.

3. Choose Properties.

4. The dialog box shown in Figure 4.4 appears. Select the desired tab, set the options you want, and click on OK.

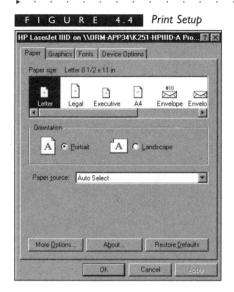

FIGURE 4.4 *Print Setup*

To print messages:

1. Select the messages you want to print.

2. Choose Print from the File menu (or press Ctrl+P).

3. Click on the Print button.

NOTE

The "Print attachment with associated application" option launches the application associated with the file attachment and prints the attachment from that application (for example, from WordPerfect). Use this option if you want to preserve the formatting of the file attachment.

Organizing Messages with the Cabinet

You use the *Cabinet* to organize and store your message folders. You can organize folders in the Cabinet the same way you organize directories in Windows 3.1, or folders in Windows 95 and on a Macintosh.

The folders in your Cabinet fall into two categories — personal folders and shared folders.

You create *personal folders* for your own, private use. Use them to organize your messages and documents into separate groups. For example, you can create folders for information pertaining to certain projects, for specific message types, or for messages from certain individuals.

You can also create shared folders. *Shared folders* contain messages that can be viewed by other users. The creator of a shared folder determines the *access rights* to the folder. For example, when you create a shared folder, you can decide who will be able to read the messages in the folder, who can add messages to that folder, and so forth.

Creating Folders

GroupWise folders work the same way as the subdirectory structure of your computer's hard drive. When you open GroupWise 5, your folders appear on the left side of the screen. Your name should automatically appear on the top-level folder (the *user folder*). In addition to your user folder, there are seven default GroupWise folders — Mailbox, Sent Items, Calendar, Task List, Work In Progress, Cabinet, and Trash.

You can only add new folders in the Cabinet, under your user folder, and under the Work In Progress folder. We recommend that you store most of your GroupWise messages in Cabinet folders. You can organize the folders and subfolders in your Cabinet however you like.

NOTE In GroupWise, folder names can include punctuation and spaces.

Figure 4.5 shows some typical folders. A button with a *plus sign* to the left of a folder indicates that the folder contains hidden subfolders. A button with a *minus sign* to the left of a folder means that the folder has been expanded to show all of its subfolders. Click on a plus or minus button to show or hide the substructure beneath a particular folder.

To create a folder:

1. If you want to create a folder that extends directly from the Cabinet folder, highlight the Cabinet folder. (If you want to create a subfolder under another folder, select the folder under which you want to create the subfolder.) You can also highlight the Work In Progress folder to create subfolders underneath it.

2. Choose File, New, and select Folder.

3. Enter the folder name and choose Next. Enter a description of the folder and choose Finish to create the folder.

As you create folders, you can change the position of a folder in the folder tree by clicking on the Move Up and Move Down buttons in the screen where you name the folder.

> **WiseGuide**
>
> To quickly create a new folder, right-click the parent folder and choose New Folder from the QuickMenu.

NOTE You can customize the appearance of the Cabinet and its folders to suit your own preferences. We explain how to customize the Cabinet and its folders in Chapter 10.

To delete a folder:

1. Select the folder to be deleted.

2. Choose Edit and then choose Delete. (Alternatively, you can right-click on the folder and choose Delete from the QuickMenu.) A summary of the messages in the folder will appear, as shown in Figure 4.6.

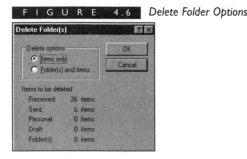

F I G U R E   4 . 6   *Delete Folder Options*

3. Choose whether to delete only the messages or both the folder and its messages.

4. Choose OK.

To rename a folder:

1. Select the folder to be renamed and then choose Rename from the Edit menu. (Alternatively, you can right-click on the folder and then choose Rename from the QuickMenu.)

2. Edit the folder name and press Enter.

TIP You can use the Folders option under the Edit menu to determine which folders open in the main GroupWise screen when you start GroupWise. You can also use this dialog box to move folders up or down in the listing of folders and to create new folders, as shown in Figure 4.7.

F I G U R E   4 . 7   *Folder Manager*

Managing Messages Using Folders

There are two different ways that you can place a message in a folder: by moving it there or by linking it to the folder. When you *move* a message to a folder, the message is actually stored in that folder.

To move a message into a folder:

1. Expand folders (if necessary) by clicking on the button with a plus sign to the left of the folder. The target folder needs to appear in the folder tree.

2. Click on the message in the Items Area and drag it into the target folder. The message will now be stored in that folder. If the message was previously stored in a different folder, it will no longer appear in that folder.

When you *link* a message to a folder, a copy of the message is placed in the destination folder. You will then see the message in the original folder *and* in the folder to which the message has been linked. Any modifications to the original message (for example, changes in the appearance of the message icon) will be reflected in the folder to which the message has been linked.

To link a message to a folder:

1. If necessary, expand folders by clicking on the plus sign to the left of the folders.

2. Hold down the Ctrl key on your keyboard, click on the message, and drag it from the original folder into the target folder. The message will now be stored in both the original folder and the folder to which the message has been linked.

You can also use the dialog box shown in Figure 4.8 to move and link your messages to folders. To access this dialog box, highlight a message and choose the Move/Link to Folders option under the Edit menu.

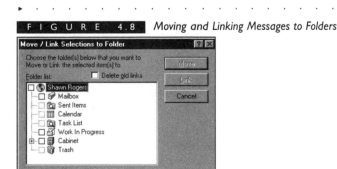

FIGURE 4.8 *Moving and Linking Messages to Folders*

Using Message Threading in a Folder

When you use *message threading*, you can view the whole history of messages and replies behind a particular message. Message threading has many uses: You can follow workflow as it develops. You can also go back and review certain steps in a long process. Figure 4.9 shows message threading.

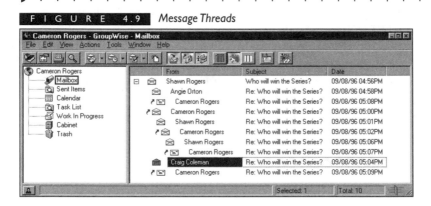

F I G U R E   4.9   *Message Threads*

To enable message threading in a folder:

1. Open a folder by clicking on it.

2. Click on View and choose Discussion Threads. (Alternatively, right-click on the Items Area and choose View Discussion Thread.)

You will now see all of the messages and their replies in a particular folder.

Sharing Folders

When you create a folder in GroupWise 5, you can easily share it (and its contents) with other people in your system. This feature, called *shared folders*, is an excellent way to manage information that pertains to many people. For example, your company might have a shared folder called "Company Notices" to store messages intended for the entire company.

As mentioned before, access to a shared folder is controlled by the creator of the folder. In the Company Notices example, a few key people might receive *Add privileges* (to add messages to the folder) and everyone else would be given *Read privileges*. Table 4.1 explains the different kinds of access privileges.

T A B L E 4.1	Access Privileges
ACCESS PRIVILEGE	**DESCRIPTION**
Read	View and read messages in a folder
Add	Add messages to a folder
Modify	Modify items in a folder
Delete	Delete items in a folder

To share a folder:

1. Highlight the folder you would like to share. (If you select a folder that has subordinate folders, only the selected folder will be shared, not the folders underneath it.)

2. Choose Sharing from the File menu. The Sharing tab opens, and the Not Shared option is highlighted.

3. Select Shared With and enter the names of the users you would like to share the folder with, or click the browse button next to the Users field to open the Address Book. If you open the Address Book, double-click on the users you would like to share this folder with. Choose Edit and then Retrieve Group if you want to share the folder with a group. Choose OK.

4. From the Sharing properties page, highlight a user from the list (or select multiple users with either Shift-click or Ctrl-click) and choose the access privileges you want the person to have. All users added to the Sharing list receive Read access by default. (*Modify* enables users to change the items in the folder, and *Delete* enables users to erase items from the folder.)

5. Choose OK.

6. A Shared Folder Notification screen appears. All new participants are displayed, and a mini message screen appears. Fill in the subject line, enter a short message, and choose OK.

Your message will automatically be sent to the participants, informing them about their access to the shared folder.

Using Filters to Manage Your Messages

You can use *filters* to screen out certain messages when viewing the stored messages in a GroupWise folder. For example, you can apply a filter to your Mailbox that displays only your Mail and Phone messages or a filter that displays only your unopened messages. You can save the filters you create and use them again later.

Here are some situations in which a filter can be very useful:

- You have a lot of messages in your Mailbox, and you want to see only unopened messages.

- You want to see only messages that were received during a specific period of time (for example, from January 1, 1996 to February 1, 1996).

- You want to see only messages you received from a specific person.

- You want to see only high-priority messages.

- You want to see only messages that contain a certain keyword in the Subject: field.

NOTE   A filter does not *remove* messages from your Mailbox; it only determines which messages are displayed. When you close a filtered display, the filter is automatically removed. The next time you open the same folder, all of the messages will appear again.

Filter Terminology

There are five key terms you should understand before you begin working with filters:

- Filter topic
- Filter qualifier
- Filter variable/constant
- Filter group
- Filter terminator

Filter Topic

The *filter topic* is the part (or parts) of a message you want considered when GroupWise determines which messages to display. The following list shows the various filter topics from which you can choose:

- Annotation
- Attachment List
- Attachments
- Author
- BC:
- Caller's Company
- Caller's Name
- Caller's Phone Number
- CC:
- Document Creator
- Document Filename
- Document Number
- Document Type
- From:
- Item Source
- Item Status
- Item Type
- Library
- Message
- Number Accepted

- Number Deleted
- Number Completed
- Number Opened
- Number Read
- Number Replied
- Place
- Priority
- Retrieved By
- Retrieved Date
- Retrieved Location
- Retrieved File
- Size
- Subject:
- To:
- Total Recipients
- Version Created Date
- Version Creator
- Version Description
- Version Number
- Version Status

Filter Qualifier

The *filter qualifier* is the logic component of a filter; it indicates the selections to be made. Each filter topic will have a different list of available qualifiers. For example, "Less Than" applies to the filter topic "Size," while "Begins With" is applicable to the filter topic "From" but not to "Size."

The following list shows the different filter qualifiers:

- Contains
- Begins With
- Matches
- Includes
- Does Not Include

- Equal To
- Not Equal To
- Less Than
- Less Than or Equal To
- Greater Than

▶ Greater Than or Equal To	▶ On or After
▶ Equal To Field	▶ After
▶ Not Equal To Field	▶ On or After Date
▶ Less Than Field	▶ On or Before
▶ Less Than or Equal to Field	▶ On Date
▶ Greater Than Field	▶ On or Before Date
▶ Greater Than or Equal to Field	▶ After Date
▶ On	▶ Before Date
▶ Before	

Filter Variable/Constant

A *filter variable* is the input on which GroupWise bases message filtering, such as a user's name. A *filter constant* sets the parameters of the filter topic. For example, "High" is a filter constant for the filter topic "Priority"; "Phone Message" is a filter constant for the filter topic "Item Type."

Filter Group

A *filter group* is a single, complete decision line in one filter. The formula for filter groups is explained in the next section, "Building a Filter."

Filter Terminator

The *filter terminator* determines what kind of action GroupWise will take once it has made the proper selections.

Table 4.2 explains the different filter terminators available.

T A B L E 4.2	*Filter Terminators*
TERMINATOR	**ACTION**
And	Adds an "And" condition to a single filter group
Or	Adds an "Or" condition to a single filter group
Insert Row	Adds an additional condition row in a single filter group
Delete Row	Deletes a condition row in a single filter group
Insert Group	Adds an additional filter group
End	Terminates the filter

Building a Filter

When you *build* a filter, you specify the criteria GroupWise will use to determine which messages to display. The formula for this decision appears in the Build Filter dialog box, as shown in Figure 4.10.

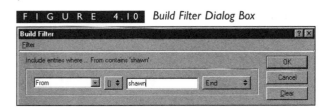

F I G U R E   4.10   *Build Filter Dialog Box*

The formula for building a filter is:

```
Include entries where <Filter topic> <Qualifier>
<Variable/Constant>
```

For example, Include entries where Item type = Phone Message will display only Phone messages in the folder.

A simple filter is a single-decision filter. A complex filter is one where multiple decisions can be evaluated. The Filter Terminator field in the far right side of the Build Filter dialog box enables you to add more than one decision.

The filter in Figure 4.11 displays only high-priority messages received from Shawn.

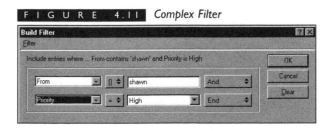

F I G U R E   4.11   *Complex Filter*

To apply a filter to a folder:

1. Open the folder, click on the View menu, and choose Filter. (Alternatively, right-click on the folder and choose Filter from the QuickMenu.)

2. Select the display criteria and choose Filter and then Save if you want to use this filter again. (You will need to specify a filename and a path in order to save the filter.)

3. Click on OK to apply the filter.

If you want to use a previously created filter:

1. Click on the View menu and then choose Filters.

2. Click on Filter, Open.

3. Select the filter you would like to use and choose OK.

The folder will now display only the filtered messages.

To return to your normal, unfiltered view, right-click in the filtered folder and choose Clear Filter from the QuickMenu.

You can use filters to locate messages. For example, if you know that John Smith sent you a message, but you can't find it among your many messages, create a filter that screens out all messages except those from John Smith.

Managing Your Outgoing Messages

The Sent Items folder contains all messages you have sent. You retain access to these messages for three purposes: to track the status of the message, to edit and resend the message, and to retract the message.

Checking the Status of Sent Items

GroupWise offers the distinctive feature of tracking the status of sent messages. With *status messages,* you can find out the disposition of any message you have sent.

You can get some information about the message simply by looking at the icon to the left of the message in the Sent Items folder. For example, if the item has not been opened by the recipient, the envelope will be closed. If the recipient has opened the message, the envelope icon is open.

Table 4.3 shows the various icons that may appear next to items in the Sent Items folder.

TABLE 4.3 *Sent Items Icons*

ICON	DESCRIPTION
😦	This icon indicates that GroupWise could not deliver the item to one or more recipients.
☒	Next to a Task, this icon indicates that at least one recipient deleted the Task without marking it complete. Next to an Appointment, the icon indicates that at least one recipient deleted or declined the Appointment without accepting it.
✓	Next to an Appointment, this icon means that not every recipient has accepted the Appointment. Next to a Task, the icon means that not every recipient has completed the Task.

The status messages in GroupWise correspond to specific message types. For example, you can check to see if a Phone message has been read or if a Task you sent has been completed. However, you can't see if an e-mail message has been completed because you can only mark a Task "Completed." Table 4.4 lists the different status messages.

TABLE 4.4 *Description of Status Messages*

STATUS	DESCRIPTION
Delivered	The message has been delivered to the recipient's Mailbox.
Opened	The message has been opened by the recipient.
Deleted	The message has been moved to the recipient's Trash.
Completed	The Task has been completed.
Accepted	The Appointment, Note, or Task has been accepted by the recipient.
Declined	The Appointment, Note, or Task has been declined by the recipient.
Transferred	The message has been transferred to the gateway.

Table 4.5 shows the different status messages that correspond to each message type.

TABLE 4.5	Message Type/Status Message Correspondence						
MESSAGE TYPE	**STATUS**						
	DELIVERED	OPENED	DELETED	ACCEPTED	DECLINED	TRANSFERRED	COMPLETED
E-Mail Message	✔	✔	✔			✔	
Phone Message	✔	✔	✔			✔	
Meeting Request	✔	✔	✔	✔	✔		
Task Assignment	✔	✔	✔	✔	✔		✔
Note	✔	✔	✔	✔	✔		

To check the status of a message:

1. Click on the Sent Items folder.
2. Double-click on the message for which you want the status. (Alternatively, you can select a message, right-click on it, and choose Properties from the QuickMenu.)

Figure 4.12 shows a typical message with a status indicator.

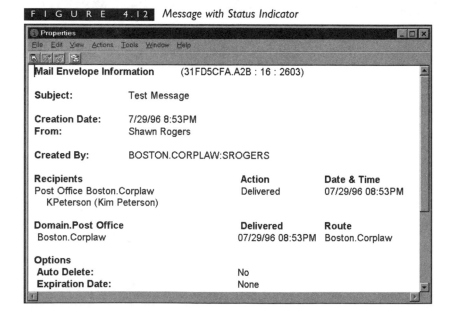

FIGURE 4.12 Message with Status Indicator

Retracting Messages

Retracting a message is extremely useful if you have regrets about a sent message, or you would otherwise like to "pull back" a message you have sent. As long as the message has not been opened, you can retract it.

IMPORTANT You cannot retract messages sent through a gateway to another mail system, such as messages you send to Internet users. You can retract a message through a gateway as long as the recipient's system is GroupWise.

To retract a message:

1. Click on the Sent Items folder.

2. Click on the message you want to retract and press the Delete key, or choose Edit and then Delete. (As a shortcut, right-click on a message and choose Delete from the QuickMenu.)

3. From the Delete Item dialog box (shown in Figure 4.13), make a choice about which Mailboxes you want to remove the message from:

   ▶ *My Mailbox* will remove the message from your Sent Items folder only, leaving a copy in the recipient's Mailbox.

   ▶ *Recipient's Mailbox* will remove the message from all recipients' Mailboxes, leaving a copy in your Sent Items folder.

   ▶ *All Mailboxes* will remove the message from all recipients' Mailboxes as well as from your Sent Items folder.

4. Choose OK and the message will be retracted.

FIGURE 4.13 *Retracting a Message*

Resending Messages

If you have ever sent a message to the president of your company only to read it later and find a glaring typo, you'll appreciate being able to resend messages with GroupWise. From the Sent Items folder, you can edit a message you have sent and resend it — with an option to retract the original message.

To resend a message:

1. Click on the Sent Items folder.

2. Click on the message you want to edit, choose Actions, and select Resend. (As a shortcut, right-click on a message and choose Resend from the QuickMenu.)

3. Edit the message, click on the Send button, and answer Yes to "Retract Original Item?", as shown in Figure 4.14.

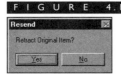

FIGURE   4.14   *Retracting the Original Message when Resending*

Managing the Trash

Do you know someone who likes to keep everything, supposing that "someday he might need it" — only to clutter up an attic or basement? Well, GroupWise is like that. Deleted messages stick around in the Trash folder until you manually empty it, or until the trash day rolls around. Trash day is set just like it is in your neighborhood, once a week. However, you can change the default setting for emptying the Trash. (We explain how to change the default setting in Chapter 10.)

You saw how to delete messages in Chapter 2. Once messages have been deleted, you can do two things to them: purge them from the Trash or undelete them.

To purge the Trash, choose Edit and then Empty Trash.

To undelete a message:

1. Highlight the Trash folder. All deleted items will appear in the Items Area.

2. Select a message or group of messages from the Items Area.

3. Select Edit and Undelete. (Alternatively, right-click on the message or group and choose Undelete from the QuickMenu.)

The message returns to its original location.

Summary

In this chapter, we explained how to use the message management features of GroupWise — archiving, saving, and printing messages; storing messages in folders; using filters; and managing the Trash. You also learned how to manage your outgoing messages with the Sent Items folder — a feature that sets GroupWise apart from other messaging systems.

CHAPTER 5

Personal Calendaring and Task Management

In this chapter, we will show you how to use GroupWise 5 to replace your old-fashioned calendar or daily planner. The time-management features of GroupWise are extraordinarily useful. Once you start using these features, you'll wonder how you ever got by without them.

When you showed up for work this morning and turned your computer on, one of your first tasks was probably to check your e-mail. After that, you probably checked your calendar to see what appointments you had for today. With GroupWise, the integration of the e-mail interface with your calendar makes it very easy to do most of your communications and scheduling with one program. As you saw in Chapter 1, switching from e-mail to your calendar is as simple as clicking on the Calendar folder.

With the Calendar's built-in views, you can instantly display Calendar items such as Appointments or Tasks. Later in this chapter, you'll learn how to change your view to one that suits your needs.

In order to use the GroupWise Calendar system most effectively, you need to understand the difference between the various Calendar items. The Calendar keeps track of three different kinds of personal reminders: Appointments, Notes, and Tasks. Table 5.1 explains the different Calendar items.

T A B L E 5.1   *Calendar Items*

ITEM	DESCRIPTION
Appointments	Personal Meetings and events on a certain date with a start time and an end time (duration)
Notes	Personal reminders for a certain date
Tasks	Project entries with a "tickle" entry in your Calendar from the start date through the due date, with a priority level

IMPORTANT

Note the distinction between Personal Calendar items and Group Calendar items. *Personal items* are not sent to anyone; you add them to your own Calendar. *Group items* are sent to other people in much the same way you send e-mail messages. (Group calendaring is discussed in Chapter 6.)

The Calendar Interface

When you click on the Calendar folder, a condensed view of your Calendar appears in the Items Area on the right side of the main GroupWise screen. This view is your Calendar folder view, as shown in Figure 5.1.

Initially, all of your Calendar items — both personal and group — appear in your Calendar. You can limit the display to only your personal items by choosing View and then Personal Items.

F I G U R E 5 . 1 *Calendar Folder View*

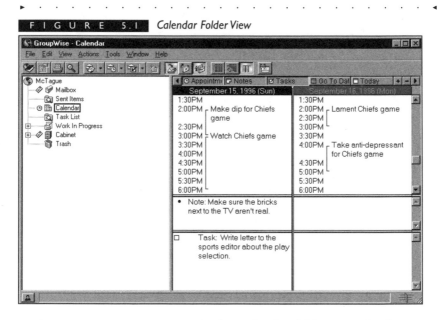

As you can see in Figure 5.1, the Calendar folder view displays your Appointments, Notes, and Tasks in separate panes in the Items Area. The subject line of each Calendar item appears. To remove or add an item in the Calendar folder view, simply click on the heading bar button (Appointments, Notes, or Tasks) for the item.

NOTE You can maximize GroupWise and see up to five days' worth of Calendar information at once in the Calendar folder view.

If you want to see the Calendar items for a different day, click on the Go to Date button on the heading bar. Type the desired date on the date line, click on the date in the month displayed, or scroll forward or back one month (single arrows), forward or back a year (double arrows) until the desired month is displayed. Figure 5.2 shows the Go to Date dialog box.

FIGURE 5.2 *Go to Date*

To quickly return to the current day's Calendar items, click on the Go to Today button on the heading bar.

TIP If you have enabled the QuickViewer, the message contents of each Calendar item will appear in the QuickViewer pane at the bottom of the screen.

Calendar Views

You can choose from 11 different views of the Calendar, including the Calendar folder view. Table 5.2 lists the different Calendar views. You'll want to experiment with them until you find the one that best suits your work style.

| TABLE 5.2 | *Calendar Views* |
NAME	FEATURES
Day	Displays Appointments, Notes, and Tasks three months at a time.
Week	Displays Appointments, Notes, and Tasks five to seven days at a time.
Year	Displays the entire year. Bold dates on the Calendar contain scheduled items, as shown in Figure 5.3.
Desk Calendar	Displays daily Appointments and Tasks one month at a time.
Notebook	Displays Notes and Tasks for one day.
Day Projects	Displays expanded Cabinet folders, Group Appointments, Tasks, and Notes — three months at a glance.
Day Planner	Displays Tasks, Appointments, and Notes — four months at a glance.
Project Planner	Displays Tasks and Notes — all folders expanded, four months at a glance, as shown in Figure 5.4.
Appt(sm)	Displays Appointments for one day.
Note (sm)	Displays Notes for one day.
Task(sm)	Displays Tasks for one day.

► · ◄

F I G U R E   5 . 3   *Year Calendar View*

► · ◄

F I G U R E   5 . 4   *Project Planner Calendar View*

To open a Calendar view:

1. Click on Window, Calendar View.
2. Click on Edit, Change To, and More.
3. Click on the desired view and click on OK.

TIP

Once you have found a view that you like, you can set that view as the default by selecting Tools, Options. If you like to use different Calendar views at different times, add the Calendar button to your Toolbar. The Calendar button provides you with one-click access to any of the Calendar views. (Setting default options and customizing the Toolbar is explained in Chapter 10.)

To change your Calendar view:

1. Choose Edit, Change To, and More.
2. Select a view from the list and click on OK.

Task List

The Task List folder contains a list of your Tasks — both personal and group. The Task List is a handy feature because you can see all of your Tasks in one place; you don't have to scan through the entire Calendar to locate them.

Notice in Figure 5.5 that you can see each Task's priority level and due date. Also note the different icons for incomplete Tasks and completed Tasks.

FIGURE 5.5 *Task List*

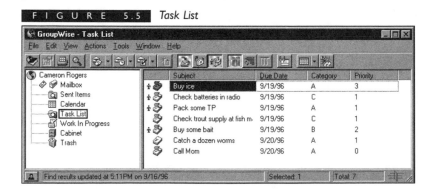

Creating Personal Appointments

A large part of time management involves scheduling appointments, and GroupWise provides an easy-to-use interface for creating and managing your personal engagements. Personal Appointment messages only appear on your Calendar; you don't send them to other people. Figure 5.6 shows an example of a Personal Appointment.

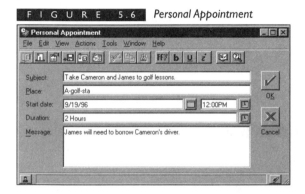

F I G U R E   5.6   *Personal Appointment*

As you can see in Figure 5.6, a Personal Appointment includes the following information: appointment date, start time, duration, and place. The time increment (default of 15 minutes) can be changed, as well as the date format. You can customize GroupWise to use military date and time as well as other formats. (See Chapter 10 for more information on customizing your GroupWise environment.) The subject line of an Appointment appears in the Calendar.

To create a Personal Appointment:

1. Click on the down arrow next to the Appointment button on the Toolbar and choose Personal Appointment from the list. Alternatively, in the Calendar view double-click on the time for which you want to make the Appointment and you will achieve the same result.

2. Enter a subject line for the Appointment and place more detailed information in the message area.

3. Fill in the Appointment date, start time, and duration, and choose OK to add the Appointment to your Calendar.

You can also set alarms for your Appointments. To set an alarm:

1. Select an Appointment and then right-click on it.

2. Choose Set Alarm from the QuickMenu. You'll see the Alarm dialog box, shown in Figure 5.7.

3. Specify in hours and minutes how much advance notice you want. The maximum is 99 hours and 59 minutes. You can also set up a variety of sounds for the alarm. (See Chapter 10 for information on how to customize the alarm.)

4. Click on OK. Notice the alarm clock icon next to the Appointment.

F I G U R E   5 . 7 *Alarm Dialog Box*

Once you set an alarm, you can change the time but you cannot remove the alarm, unless you delete the Appointment.

NOTE

Creating Personal Tasks

Personal Tasks are very useful, reminding you to finish assignments or projects that may last for several days. As you saw earlier in this chapter, your Tasks appear in the Task List folder in the main GroupWise screen.

Each Task has a start date, an end date, and a priority level, as shown in Figure 5.8. The priority level determines the order in which the Tasks appear in the list, based on an alphabetic and numeric code. For example, a Task with a priority of A1 appears before A2, and A2 appears before B1. The code you assign to a Task is completely up to you. You can use only letters or only numbers if you prefer.

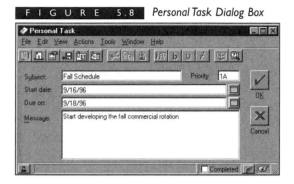

FIGURE 5.8 *Personal Task Dialog Box*

The subject line of each Task you create appears on the starting day's Calendar, and will carry forward each day until you mark the Task Completed check box. If a Task is not marked completed by the due date, it will continue to be carried forward, but it will appear red in the Task List.

To create a Personal Task:

1. Click on the arrow next to the Task button on the Toolbar and choose Personal Task from the list.

2. Enter a subject line for the Task. You can place more detailed information in the message area.

3. Enter a priority level for the Task (or leave the priority setting blank if you like).

4. Enter a start date (which must be today's date or later) and an end date.

5. Choose OK to enter the Task in your Calendar.

WiseGuide

You can also double-click in the Task pane of the Calendar folder to create a Personal Task.

To mark a Task completed, click on the Task heading button in the Calendar folder. Click on the box next to the Task in the Task list. Notice that a check mark appears in the box.

Creating Personal Notes

Personal Notes can be added to your Calendar and tied to certain dates as reminders, as shown in Figure 5.9. The subject line of each Note appears in your Calendar. You can use Personal Notes to remind yourself about anything you like — for example, picking up your dry cleaning. You might also use a recurring Note to mark paydays on your Calendar.

FIGURE 5.9 *Personal Note Dialog Box*

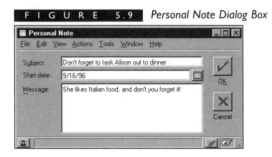

To create a Personal Note:

1. Click on the Notes heading button in the Calendar folder, and then double-click on the Note pane under your Appointments.

2. Enter a subject line for the Note. If you like, you can place details about the Note in the message area.

3. Fill in the date for the Note and choose OK to add the Note to your Calendar.

Rescheduling Appointments, Tasks, and Notes

Rescheduling an Appointment, Task, or Note only requires a simple click and drag of the mouse.

To move an Appointment, Task, or Note to a different day:

1. Open your Calendar folder.

2. If the day you need to move the item to does not appear, open the Day view of the Calendar. (See the "Calendar Views" section at the beginning of this chapter for instructions on changing views.) The Day view displays three months at a glance.

3. Click on the Appointment, Task, or Note you want to reschedule and drag it to the new day.

To change the time of a Personal Appointment:

1. Open your Calendar folder and single-click on the Appointment you want to change.

2. With the mouse button held down, drag the Appointment to a new time on the same day, and the Appointment will move.

Summary

In this chapter, you have seen the many features of GroupWise as they relate to your own calendar. The Appointments, Notes, and Tasks that you create to manage your time can also be used to invite people to meetings, remind them of events on a certain day, and to delegate tasks. The next chapter shows you how to make the most of the GroupWise 5 group scheduling and workflow features.

CHAPTER 6

Group Calendaring and Task Management

In Chapter 5, you learned how to manage your personal Calendar items, such as Appointments and Tasks. In Chapter 6, we show you how to use the GroupWise 5 workgroup features, including group calendaring and task management.

Scheduling Meetings

When you want to schedule a meeting with other people, you send an *Appointment message.*

NOTE

Appointment messages that you send to other people are sometimes referred to as *Meetings* or *Meeting Requests.*

In some cases you may need to schedule a meeting for someone else, such as your supervisor. GroupWise enables you to schedule meetings for others (in other words, meetings that you don't plan to attend).

TIP

You can use the GroupWise *Proxy* feature to view and manage others' Calendars. (Chapter 7 explains the Proxy feature.)

Sending Appointments

You send Appointments to other GroupWise users to schedule meetings — either for yourself or for someone else. When you want to send an Appointment, you must set a start date, a start time, and a duration — just like you do for Personal Appointments. The only difference is that you are sending the Appointment request to others, not just adding the Appointment to your Calendar.

To create and send an Appointment:

1. Click on File, New, and Appointment.

2. Address the Appointment message just as you would any other type of GroupWise message — by entering the names in the To: field or by using the Address Book. If you plan to attend the meeting, *make sure you include your own name in the To: field.* If you do not include your own name, the Appointment will not appear in your Calendar. (By default, GroupWise inserts your name in the To: field when you create an Appointment.)

3. Enter the location of the meeting in the Place: field.

TIP

If your system administrator has made the meeting place (for example, a certain conference room) a *resource*, you can schedule the room at the same time you send the Appointment. Open the Address Book, click on View, Predefined Filters, and Resources. Select the room from the list of resources. If the room has not been defined as a resource, you can describe the meeting place in the Place: field, but the room will not be reserved.

4. Enter a subject in the subject line. (Be descriptive because only the subject line appears in the recipients' Calendars.)

5. Enter detailed information about the meeting in the Message: field. If you like, you can attach a file such as a meeting agenda. (If you attach a file, mention the attachment in the Message: field. Because the Appointment view does not contain a file attachment field, recipients must access the attachment with the attachment icon at the bottom of the message or by going to the File menu. For more information about viewing and saving attachments, see Chapter 4.)

6. Set the date of the meeting by typing the date in the Start Date: field or by clicking on the small calendar icon to the right of that field.

NOTE

If you want to create a recurring Appointment, you can use the Auto-Date feature, explained later in this chapter.

7. Set the time of the meeting by typing the time in the field to the right of the small calendar icon or by clicking on the small clock icon next to that field.

8. Enter the duration of the meeting in the Duration: field (or set the duration by clicking on the small clock icon to the right of the Duration: field).

9. Choose Send.

The Appointment appears in the recipients' Mailboxes and Calendars. When you schedule meetings, you can use the Busy Search feature to find a time when all attendees are available. The *Busy Search* feature automatically sets the date, time, and duration of the meeting. Busy Searches are explained in the next section.

Busy Searching

The Busy Search feature is a very powerful GroupWise scheduling tool. You no longer need to call people in advance of a meeting to find a time when everyone can meet. GroupWise takes care of that chore for you.

To perform a Busy Search when scheduling a meeting:

1. Open a new Appointment message and use the Address Book to place the attendees' addresses in the To: field.

2. Click the Busy? button in the lower right corner of the message box. GroupWise searches the users' Calendars and displays the Choose Appointment Time dialog box, as shown in Figure 6.1.

FIGURE 6.1 *Busy Search Dialog Box Showing Individual Schedules*

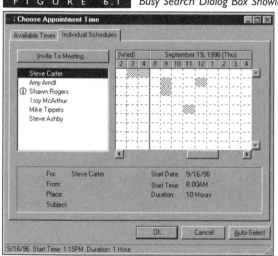

The Choose Appointment Time dialog box presents you with a grid showing you the schedule of each user you specified. An empty space across from the user name indicates that the user is available for that time.

If you want GroupWise to show you the times when all users are available, click on the Available Times tab. The dialog box shown in Figure 6.2 appears.

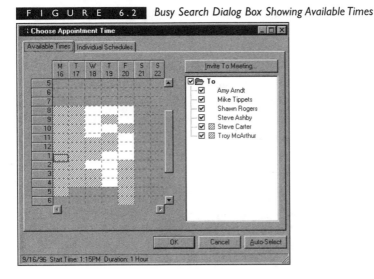

F I G U R E   6.2 *Busy Search Dialog Box Showing Available Times*

You can select the Appointment time from either of the Choose Appointment Time screens. To set the Appointment time:

1. Click on the highlighted box in the grid and drag it to a time the attendees are available. You can click and drag on the sides of this box to increase or decrease the duration of the meeting.

2. Click on OK. The date and time of the meeting appear in the appropriate fields of the Appointment message.

Here are some handy Busy Search tips:

▶ To include more users in the Busy Search from the Choose Appointment Time dialog box, click on the Invite To Meeting button.

▶ If there isn't a time when all attendees are free, you can extend the search to include more days by clicking the Invite To Meeting button and increasing the value in the Number Of Days To Search field.

▶ When the Choose Appointment Time dialog box shows that some users are busy, you can find out what a user has scheduled by clicking on the box representing that time slot. (You can see the person's schedule only if the user has granted you access rights to his or her Calendar.)

▶ The Auto-Select button selects a time when all of the selected users are free for the duration you have specified.

- You can exclude a user from the Busy Search without removing the user from the To: field by choosing the Available Times tab and then clearing the check mark that appears next to the user's name in the right side of the dialog box. (This exclusion feature is useful when someone should be invited but it is not absolutely necessary for that person to attend.)

- To perform a Busy Search before creating your Appointment message, choose Tools and then Busy Search. Enter the users in the dialog box that appears.

- You can add names to the Busy Search by clicking on the Invite To Meeting button. You can delete names from the Busy Search by clicking on the user name and pressing the Delete key.

- If you are Busy Searching for multiple users, GroupWise may take awhile to return the results on all users. You can minimize the Busy Search dialog box and work on other tasks while GroupWise receives the Busy Search results. A status box will appear on your Windows Taskbar showing you the search progress.

- You can do a Busy Search for a resource (such as a conference room, a company car, or a VCR) to find out times when the resource is not reserved.

To change Busy Search defaults:

1. Click on Tools and then on Options.
2. Double-click on the Date and Time icon.
3. Choose the Busy Search tab.

IMPORTANT

The Busy Search feature is only useful if all GroupWise users keep their Calendars up to date.

Sending Tasks

Use GroupWise Task messages for assigning projects to other GroupWise users. Tasks are also useful for large projects that involve many people.

To send a Task:

1. Choose File, New.
2. Select Task. The Task message shown in Figure 6.3 appears.

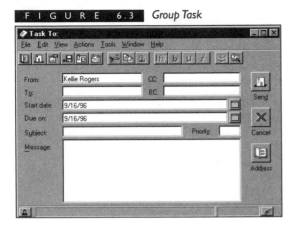

FIGURE 6.3 Group Task

3. Address the Task message by typing in the recipient's name or by using the Address Book.

4. Enter a priority code for the Task. The Task priority can be a character, a number, or a character followed by a number. For example, these are valid priority codes: A, B, C, 1, 2, 3, A1, B1, B2, and so on.

5. Enter the subject and message in the appropriate fields.

6. Select a start date. The start date is the date when the Task will first appear in the recipient's Calendar, after the recipient accepts the Task from his or her Mailbox.

7. Select a due date. Tasks that are not completed before the due date turn red in the recipient's Calendar.

8. Choose Send.

In addition to the priority code you enter in the Task message screen, you can also set a priority for the message:

1. Choose File.

2. Select Properties.

3. Choose the Send Options tab.

4. Select High, Normal, or Low priority from the Priority: field.

5. Choose OK.

Sending Notes

Use Group Notes to send reminders to people. Group Notes are very use-ful as meeting reminders because Notes appear on specific days in the recipi-ents' Calendars. Often, Notes are used to remind others about specific assignments for upcoming meetings.

To send a Group Note:

1. Select File, New.
2. Select Note.
3. Enter the information in the To:, Subject:, and Message: fields.
4. Specify a date for the Note in the Start Date: field.
5. Choose Send.

Figure 6.4 shows a typical Group Note.

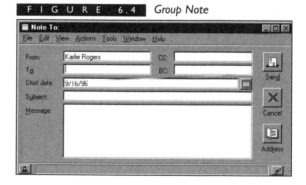

FIGURE 6.4 *Group Note*

Monitoring Appointments, Tasks, and Notes

Users often fail to keep their Calendars up to date, and even though a Busy Search may show that they are available, they may not be. After you send the Appointment, you should monitor the status of the message to find out if it has been accepted, declined, or delegated (or simply ignored).

If a recipient has declined the message and has provided a comment explaining why, that comment appears in the message status information, *not* as a message in your Mailbox. (See Chapter 4 for more information on check-ing the status of sent items.)

To see whether the recipients have accepted, declined, or delegated a message, and to view their comments:

1. Open your Sent Items folder.

2. Double-click on the Appointment message to see the status, or right-click on the message and choose Properties.

Retracting Appointments, Tasks, and Notes

Unlike regular e-mail messages, you can retract Appointments, Tasks, and Notes *after* the recipients have opened them. When you retract an Appointment, Task, or Note, it is removed from the recipients' Calendars and Mailboxes.

To retract an Appointment, Task, or Note:

1. Open your Sent Items folder and highlight the message to be retracted.

2. Press the Delete key (or right-click on the message and select Delete).

3. Select Recipient's Mailbox or All Mailboxes and click on OK.

To reschedule or resend a Calendar entry:

1. Right-click on the message in the Sent Items folder and select Resend.

2. Change the message information, if necessary, and click on Send.

3. If you want to retract the original entry, choose Yes when prompted.

Because the recipients receive no warning (the item simply disappears from their Calendars), it is good messaging etiquette to let them know you have retracted an item.

Receiving Appointments, Tasks, and Notes

The Appointments, Tasks, and Notes that you receive from other GroupWise users appear in your Mailbox along with other e-mail messages. Appointments, Tasks, and Notes also appear in your Calendar folder or in your Calendar view on the specified date. In the Calendar they appear in italics with a pencil icon until you accept them, indicating that the item has been "penciled in" but not formally accepted.

Figure 6.5 shows an opened Calendar folder with accepted and unaccepted

Appointments, Tasks, and Notes.

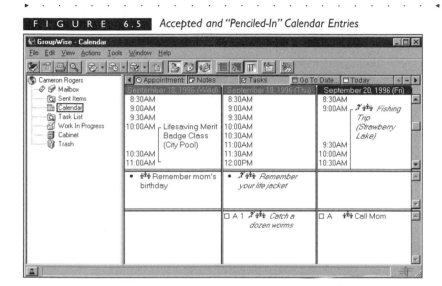

FIGURE 6.5 *Accepted and "Penciled-In" Calendar Entries*

You have several options when you receive an Appointment, Task, or Note from someone else. You can accept the entry, and it will convert the penciled-in entry to a regular (non-italicized) entry. Alternatively, you can decline the message, and it will move to your Trash folder.

Accepting

To accept an Appointment, Task, or Note, from the Mailbox or Calendar folder, double-click on the icon to open it and choose the Accept button (or right-click on the item and choose Accept from the QuickMenu).

Declining

To decline an Appointment, Task, or Note, from the Mailbox or Calendar folder, double-click on the icon to open it and choose the Decline button (or right-click on the item and choose Decline from the QuickMenu). When you decline an entry, you are given the option to comment about why you have declined. If you enter a comment, the sender can see it when he or she checks the status of the message you declined.

Delegating

If you receive an Appointment that you cannot attend or a Task you cannot complete, but you desire that someone else attend in your place or complete the Task, you can delegate the message.

When you delegate an Appointment or Task, you pass it along to someone else without necessarily keeping a copy for yourself. To delegate an Appointment or Task, right-click on the item and choose Delegate from the QuickMenu.

To delegate an Appointment or Task when the item is open:

1. Select Actions.

2. Select Delegate. A new message is created, identical to the message you received, except that the word "Delegated" is appended to the subject line.

3. Address the message to the person to whom it is being delegated.

4. Choose Send. You will be asked if you want to keep a copy of the item in your Mailbox.

5. Answer Yes or No.

The person who sent you the message can find out that you have delegated the item by checking the message status. The "Delegated" status will appear along with the name of the person to whom you delegated the Appointment or Task.

Using Auto-Date

The GroupWise Auto-Date feature enables you to send recurring Appointments, Tasks, or Note messages. Auto-Date enables you to send one message that applies to many different days. For example, you can use an Appointment Auto-Date to schedule a staff meeting that occurs every Wednesday at 9:00 a.m. Or you can use a Task Auto-Date to make sure staff members turn in a report on a certain day each month. You can also send a Note configured with Auto-Dates to remind employees when it is payday.

There are three different ways to create Auto-Date messages:

- By Dates
- By Example
- By Formula

NOTE For the most part, the By Example method makes the By Formula method obsolete. Therefore, we do not discuss the By Formula option.

By Dates

The *By Dates* Auto-Date method is the easiest to use and understand. When you choose this method, a calendar opens up for the current year and you click the dates on which you want the Appointment, Task, or Note to appear. You can click on the Year button to advance the calendar to the next year.

To create an Auto-Date Calendar entry using the By Dates method:

1. Open a new Appointment, Task, or Note message.

2. Fill in the To:, Subject:, and Message: fields.

3. Click on the Actions pull-down menu.

4. Select Auto-Date. The Auto-Date dialog box appears, as shown in Figure 6.6. (The Dates tab is active by default.)

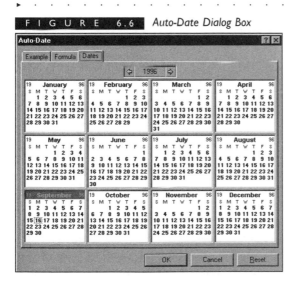

F I G U R E   6.6   *Auto-Date Dialog Box*

5. Click on all dates when the Appointment, Task, or Note should appear.

6. Choose OK.

7. Choose Send to send the message.

By Example

Use the *By Example* Auto-Date method when you want to send Appointments, Tasks, or Notes for dates that follow a regular pattern. For instance, a By Example Auto-Date could be used to schedule a meeting that occurs on the third Tuesday of every month.

The By Example Auto-Date requires some experimenting to get the hang of it. The following example should help you get a sense of how it works.

One of the most common ways people use Auto-Date is to create Personal Notes reminding themselves when it's payday. The following steps show how to use Auto-Date to create a Personal Note for a payday that occurs on the first and fifteenth day of every month, unless the payday falls on a weekend. If the first or fifteenth falls on a weekend, the payday occurs on the preceding Friday. Here is what you would do:

1. Click on Window.

2. Click on Calendar view to see your personal Calendar.

3. Double-click in the Notes field to open the Personal Note message.

4. Click on Actions.

5. Click on Auto-Date.

6. Choose the Example tab.

7. In the Start: field, enter the day when the Auto-Date period should begin.

8. In the End field, enter the date when the Auto-Date period should end.

9. Click on all months in the Months field to indicate that the paydays occur every month.

10. Click on the drop-down list box named Days of the Week and select instead the Days of the Month setting. The dialog box changes to enable you to specify certain days in the month for the Note.

11. Highlight Monday, Tuesday, Wednesday, Thursday, and Friday to indicate that the Note should only appear on a weekday.

12. Choose On/Before from the drop-down list located below the days you have highlighted. The On/Before option tells GroupWise that the Note can only appear on or before the day you specify. For example, if the 15th falls on a Saturday, the Note should appear on the previous Friday.

13. Click on 1 and 15 in the calendar to indicate the dates when the Note should appear. Figure 6.7 shows how the Auto-Date dialog box should look at this point.

14. Click on OK.

15. Fill in the remaining message fields and choose Send.

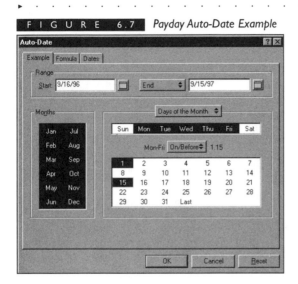

F I G U R E   6.7   *Payday Auto-Date Example*

A Note will appear in your Calendar on each day that meets the Auto-Date criteria during the period you specified in the date range fields.

When you send an Appointment message or Note created using Auto-Date, one message is created and sent by the GroupWise system for every date that meets the Auto-Date criteria. If you send an Auto-Date Appointment message that occurs every Friday during a year interval, 56 separate Appointments will appear in each recipient's Mailbox. The recipient will be given the option to accept all instances at once or to accept or decline each message individually.

The online help system includes a guide for using the Auto-Date feature. To access the guide:

1. Click on Help.

2. Click on Guides.

3. Choose the Learning the Basics option.

4. Select the "Scheduling a recurring event" guide.

Summary

In this chapter you learned how to use the powerful GroupWise group calendaring and task-management features.

In Chapter 7, you will learn about some of the advanced workgroup features that will increase your ability to collaborate with others using GroupWise.

CHAPTER 7

Advanced
Features

In this chapter, we introduce you to the advanced features of GroupWise: rules, proxies, sending options, and discussions. We also explain how to modify the look of your messages — by changing the font, text color, and text attributes — and how to embed OLE objects in your messages.

Rules enable you to automate your message management. With rules, you can have GroupWise automatically perform a wide variety of tasks, such as replying to or forwarding messages, accepting Appointments, and moving messages into designated folders.

With the *Proxy* feature, you can view other people's messages or Calendar information (provided you have been granted the necessary rights) or enable coworkers to enter Appointments into your own Calendar.

Much like you can choose next-day or second-day delivery for a package, or a delivery receipt for a certified letter, you can specify many *sending options* for your GroupWise messages. In addition, you can alter the appearance of messages by adjusting fonts, color, and attributes to express your personality through your e-mail.

The *Discussions* feature adds a very productive workflow capability to GroupWise. A discussion is used to gather related messages in one area and share them with a group of people (through shared folders). The progression of messages can be viewed as a "thread" in the Discussion Area, much like an Internet bulletin board.

Finally, you'll learn how to create messages that "activate": Imagine creating a message that says "Click here to update your sales spreadsheet." In the center of the message is a large button that, when clicked on, automatically copies an updated spreadsheet to the recipient's hard drive. Adding *OLE objects* to your messages enables you to do this and much more.

Automating GroupWise with Rules

GroupWise has the capability of managing most of your messages for you (even while you are not logged into the system) through GroupWise *rules*. Rules enable you to move messages to folders, generate automatic replies, forward messages, and delete messages. You can also set up rules to automatically manage your Calendar items. For example, you can create a rule that accepts all Tasks your boss sends you (always a good idea) or that automatically declines Appointments scheduled after 5:00 p.m. (an even better idea).

WiseGuide

Your workstation computer does not store or run your rules. Rules are stored on the network and run by a program called the Post Office Agent. Storage on the network means that rules can be executed even when you're not logged on to the network.

In this chapter, we won't try to list all of the possible rules you can create, but we will explain the basics for setting up rules. We'll also show you a few useful examples.

To create a rule:

1. Select Rules from the Tools menu and then choose New. The Rules dialog box shown in Figure 7.1 appears.

2. Fill in the fields and choose Save.

The example rule created in Figure 7.1 moves all High Priority messages to a folder named "Important Mail."

F I G U R E   7.1 *The Rules Dialog Box*

The rule is added to your *Rule List* and is automatically activated. (The red check mark in the box next to a rule indicates that the rule is activated.) Your Rule List shows all of the rules you have saved — both active and inactive, as shown in Figure 7.2.

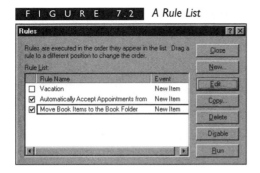

A Rule List

To modify a rule: Click on the rule and then on the Edit button. You can then change any of the parameters of the rule. Choose Save to complete your changes to the rule.

To copy or delete a rule: Click on the rule and then choose either the Copy button or the Delete button. You can use the Copy feature to create additional rules, based on the original rule. For example, if you create a rule that routes all message from a specific user to a specific folder, you could copy this rule for messages from another user that you want routed to a different folder.

To activate or deactivate a rule: Click on the check box next to the rule or use the Enable/Disable button to the right of the Rule List.

To run a rule: Click on the rule in the list and then click on the Run button. You only need to use the Run button when you create a new rule that will act upon messages already in your Mailbox.

Figures 7.3 through 7.5 show the details of three commonly used rules:

▶ A vacation rule that will automatically reply to the sender and forward the message to someone

▶ A rule that automatically accepts Appointments from a certain person

▶ A rule that moves messages to a folder automatically, based on the subject of the message

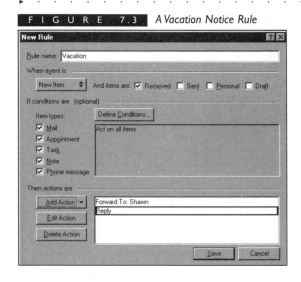

FIGURE 7.3 *A Vacation Notice Rule*

FIGURE 7.4 *An Appointment-Accepting Rule*

FIGURE 7.5 *A Message-Filing Rule*

Using the Proxy Feature

The Proxy feature enables you to access other users' GroupWise messages and Calendars. This feature also enables you to let others view your GroupWise messages.

NOTE

Remember, your Mailbox contains all of your GroupWise information: e-mail messages, Calendar items, sent items, deleted messages, personal folders, rules, and so forth.

Depending on how your administrator has configured your GroupWise system, your Proxy feature may not apply to all other GroupWise users. Ask your system administrator if your Proxy feature is limited to only users within your post office.

There are two general steps in setting up a Proxy session:

► Specifying access to a Mailbox — who can access what information, and how (Read? Write? Both?)

▶ Starting a Proxy session — the process of opening up someone else's
Mailbox

Remember, you cannot access others' Mailboxes until they have given you access privileges to their Mailboxes. Likewise, others cannot access your Mailbox until you have granted them access privileges.

IMPORTANT

Be sure you completely understand the available access privileges before granting them to others. If you are too liberal when you grant rights to your Mailbox, other users can send messages as if they were you.

Allowing Access to Your Mailbox

You control all access to your Mailbox. Others cannot access your Mailbox unless you first grant them rights. The first thing you need to do is set a password on your Mailbox (if you haven't already). Next, you need to grant access for any of the three following areas:

▶ Mail and Phone messages

▶ Calendar items (Appointments, Notes, and Tasks)

▶ Notifications, Preferences, and Private Items (Private Items are explained later in this chapter.)

Setting a Password

To provide the highest level of security for your Mailbox, we strongly recommend setting a password. You shouldn't tell anyone your password unless he or she needs to have access to your Mailbox.

NOTE

Setting a password is an option you establish through the Tools menu. (We discuss how to set other options and defaults in Chapter 10.)

To set a password on your Mailbox:

1. Select Options from the Tools menu and double-click on the Security icon.

2. Enter a password in the New Password field and in the Confirm New Password field. Choose OK to set the password. The next time you start GroupWise, you will need to type in your password.

Your password is case-sensitive and is unknown to the administrator or anyone else. If you forget your password, the administrator can reset it.

Granting Access to Others

To grant other GroupWise users access rights to your Mailbox:

1. From the Tools menu, choose Options, and double-click on the Security icon.

2. Choose the Proxy Access tab.

3. Click on the Address Book button next to the Name: field to start the Address Book. Double-click on the user you want to grant access to. Choose OK to add the user to the access list.

Minimum User Access assigns rights to any GroupWise user that can access your Mailbox. Depending upon the system configuration, this may be any user in the entire GroupWise system. Use caution when making this choice.

4. With the user in the Access List highlighted, select the appropriate access. (Refer to Table 7.1 for a description of the access rights.) Choose OK and Close to apply the rights.

5. To remove a user from the Access List, highlight the user in the Access List and click on the Remove User button.

6. To change someone's access, highlight the user in the Access List, change the rights, click on OK, and Close to complete the change.

TABLE 7.1	*Proxy Access Fields*
ACCESS RIGHT	**DESCRIPTION**
Mail/Phone	*Read:* Read messages in your Mailbox folder.
	Write: Write e-mail and phone messages in your stead.
Appointments	*Read:* Read Personal and Group Appointments from Calendar.
	Write: Create Personal Appointments and invite others to meetings in your stead.

(continued)

TABLE 7.1	Proxy Access Fields (continued)
ACCESS RIGHT	**DESCRIPTION**
Reminder Notes	*Read:* Read Personal and Accepted Notes from Calendar.
	Write: Create Personal Notes and send Notes in your stead.
Tasks	*Read:* Read Personal Tasks and Assigned Tasks from your Calendar or To Do List.
	Write: Create Personal Tasks or send Tasks to others in your stead.
Subscribe to My Alarms	Enable users to have alarms for your Appointments displayed on their computers.
Subscribe to My Notifications	Enable users to have notifications for all messages you receive displayed on their computers.
Modify Preferences/ Rules/Groups	Enable users to change your preferences (password, Mailbox access, defaults, etc.), create rules for your Mailbox, and add Personal Groups to your Address Book.
Archive Items	Enable users to archive any of your messages or Calendar items to their archive files.
Read Items Marked Private	Enable users to read any item (Mail message, Appointment, Task, or Note) that is marked Private.

IMPORTANT

You should only grant *Modify Preferences* rights to very trustworthy individuals. These rights enable users to change your password and grant others access to your Mailbox.

Starting a Proxy Session

With the Proxy feature, you can access a person's *entire* Mailbox with the permissions he or she has given you. Having full access to someone else's Mailbox does not simply mean you can view the person's messages and Calendar items. In addition to those areas, you can access the person's Sent Items, personal folders in the Cabinet, deleted messages in Trash, and the person's rules and preferences. In effect, you *become* the person who gives you access privileges.

After you are through viewing someone else's Mailbox, you need to start another Proxy session to view your Mailbox again. If you like, you can open an additional GroupWise window for the other user, while keeping your Mailbox open. We explain this technique in more detail later in this chapter. To start a Proxy session and view someone else's Mailbox:

1. Click on the Proxy icon in the lower left corner of any GroupWise folder, as shown in Figure 7.6. To view someone else's Mailbox, choose the Proxy option from this menu.

2. Type in the User ID of the user whose Mailbox you want to access, or click on the Address Book icon next to Name: field. Double-click on the user from the Address Book and choose OK. You may need to choose the Novell GroupWise Address Book tab to see the list of network users.

3. If the "target" user has a password on his or her Mailbox, you will be prompted for it. After the correct password is entered, the Proxy session starts. Note that the last name of the user whose Mailbox you are accessing appears in the GroupWise title bar, as shown in Figure 7.6.

F I G U R E   7.6   *Proxy Session*

Proxy Session Title Bar

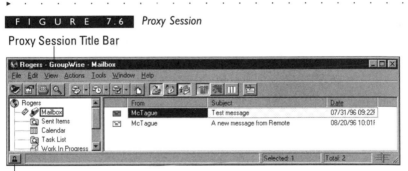

Proxy Icon

To end the session and view your Mailbox again, click on the Proxy icon at the lower left-hand corner of the main GroupWise screen and click on your name on the list. Your Mailbox will open.

Opening Multiple Windows

By default, your main GroupWise window will change to the Mailbox you are accessing with the Proxy feature. This default can be tedious if you need to view multiple Mailboxes. However, you can open a different GroupWise window for each active Proxy session. This multiple-window feature enables you to view many different Mailboxes and Calendars from your workstation.

TIP There are other reasons to open multiple GroupWise windows. For example, you can have one window viewing the new messages in your Mailbox, another one showing your open Calendar, and a third window viewing documents in the document library.

To open an extra GroupWise window (with your Mailbox open):

1. From the Window menu, choose Open New Window. A new, complete GroupWise window appears on your screen.

2. Click on the "Proxy" icon in the lower left-hand corner of this new window and start a Proxy session with another Mailbox. This new window displays the Mailbox you are accessing.

3. You can access any of the open windows by choosing that window from the Window menu. Each window is labeled with the last name of the user whose Mailbox is open.

Send Options

When you create any type of message — from Mail messages to Tasks — you can specify a number of different *send options* (in other words, options that affect the way GroupWise sends the message). We categorize these options into three categories: general options, advanced options, and mark private.

To apply one of the send options to a message you are creating:

1. Choose the Properties option under the File menu before you choose Send. The main message option screen appears, as shown in Figure 7.7.

2. The general options are displayed by clicking on the Send Options tab. Choose the Advanced Send Options tab to display the advanced options.

3. Select the desired options, and click on OK to apply the options. The message will be sent with the chosen options.

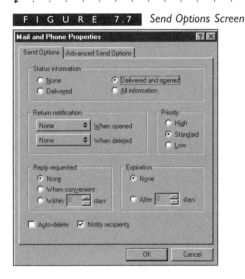

FIGURE 7.7 *Send Options Screen*

NOTE

You can set any of these send options as the default. (Setting defaults is covered in Chapter 10.)

General Options

Table 7.2 summarizes the general options.

TABLE 7.2	General Send Options	
OPTION	AVAILABLE CHOICES	DESCRIPTION
Status Information	None	No status information for this message
	Delivered	Status for delivered date and time
	*Delivered and Open	Status for delivered and opened
	All Information	Delivered, Opened, Deleted (E-Mail)
		Delivered, Accepted, Declined (Appointments)
		Delivered, Accepted, Declined, Completed, Deleted (Tasks)
		Delivered, Accepted, Declined, Deleted (Notes)
Return Notification (When Opened or When Deleted)	*None	No notification or Mail
	Mail Receipt	New message in Mailbox
	Notify	Notification
	Notify and Mail	Notification and new message in Mailbox
Priority	High	Delivered before other messages
	*Standard	Normal Delivery
	Low	Deliver after Standard priority messages
Reply Requested	*None	No reply requested
	When Convenient	Reply is requested when convenient
	Within n days	Reply requested within n days (up to 99)

(continued)

Expiration	*None	Message deleted from Mailbox by the recipient
	After *n* days	Message deleted from Mailbox after *n* days (up to 250)
Auto Delete	On/Off	Delete the message from the sender's Sent Items folder after all recipients have deleted it from their Mailboxes
Notify Recipients	On/Off	Use the Notify program to tell recipients that this message has been delivered

*Denotes default option

Advanced Options

Table 7.3 explains the advanced send options.

TABLE 7.3	Advanced Send Options	
OPTION	**AVAILABLE CHOICES**	**DESCRIPTION**
Item Options	*Create Sent Item	Enter message into the Sent Items folder
	Conceal Subject	Do not display the subject to the recipient in the Mailbox (Note: The subject appears when the message is read.)
	Deliver after *n* days	Delay message delivery for *n* days
	Deliver on *date/time*	Delay message delivery until specified *date* and *time*

(continued)

TABLE 7.3	Advanced Send Options (continued)	
OPTION	AVAILABLE CHOICES	DESCRIPTION
Security	*Normal	No Security heading in message
	Proprietary	"Proprietary" heading
	Confidential	"Confidential" heading
	Secret	"Secret" heading
	Top Secret	"Top Secret" heading
	For Your Eyes Only	"For Your Eyes Only" heading
Convert Attachments	On/Off	Convert file attachments that pass through a gateway

*Denotes default option

Mark Private

Sometimes you want to put information in your Calendar that is so private you don't want even your closest proxy associates to see it. You just want them to know you are busy. An extra measure of control on any item in your Mailbox — e-mail messages, Appointments, Tasks, Notes, or any other message — is marking the item "Private". Marking the item Private does not change the way GroupWise handles the message, but it does place a "lock" on the item.

You want to mark items Private when you have granted others access to your Mailbox. Unless you grant them the right called Read Items Marked Private, any item you mark as Private will be invisible to them.

To mark an item Private, simply highlight the item and choose the Mark Private option from the Actions menu.

NOTE   If the item being marked as Private is a Calendar item, a padlock icon appears next to the item. If it is any other kind of item, no indication is given that the item is Private, except for a check mark next to the Mark Private option under the Actions menu.

To remove the Private setting, highlight the item and choose the Mark Private option under the Actions menu. This action will remove the check mark.

Discussions

In GroupWise terminology, a *discussion* is an advanced message type that enables related messages to appear under one umbrella, called a *Discussion Area*. You can view the history of people's thought processes and the flow of their messages in a Discussion Area by using the *Discussion Thread* option under the View menu.

Discussion Areas and discussion messages are created, stored, and accessed through shared folders. For more information about shared folders, see Chapter 4.

To create a new Discussion Area:

1. Highlight a shared folder in the Folders Area.

2. Choose New from the File menu. Select Discussion from the list of message types.

3. Enter a subject line and message body, and attach a file if you wish by clicking on the paper clip at the bottom of the New Discussion screen, as shown in Figure 7.8.

4. Click on OK to place the new discussion in the shared folder.

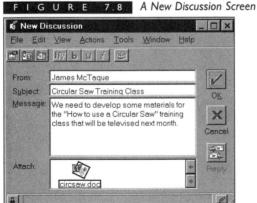

F I G U R E   7 . 8   *A New Discussion Screen*

To read and reply to a discussion message:

1. Highlight a shared folder in the Folders Area.

2. Choose View and Discussion Thread. The discussions in this folder will appear, along with the replies.
3. Double-click on the discussion or reply you wish to read.
4. To create a reply, click on Reply. You'll see the dialog box shown in Figure 7.9.

NOTE

If someone is currently creating a reply to a discussion message, no one else can read the discussion message until the reply is complete.

FIGURE 7.9 *Replying to a Discussion*

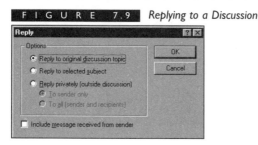

If you would like to post a reply in the Discussion Area, choose either "Reply to selected subject" or "Reply to original discussion topic" in the Reply dialog box. Your reply will appear under the appropriate message.

If you would like to reply to any part of a discussion and not include your reply in the shared folder, select "Reply privately (outside discussion)" and send your reply either to the sender only or to all participants in the discussion.

Discussions are useful for quickly sharing information with a large group of people and for achieving smooth workflow. Discussions also provide a public, recorded history of communications at your organization.

Appearance Options

As you are typing a message, you may decide you want to change the appearance of the text. You can change the appearance by choosing from the various *appearance options*. You can enlarge the font (type size), change the color, or make characters bold or italic.

To change the appearance of a message:

1. Select the text to be formatted by left-clicking on the first character of the first word and drag the mouse, while holding down the mouse button, to the end of the last word. Release the mouse button, and notice that the selected text is highlighted. (Alternatively, hold down the Shift key and use the arrow keys to move the cursor and highlight the text.)

2. Choose Edit and Font, which opens a small submenu. To make the text bold, italic, underline or normal (remove formatting), click on your selection from this menu. (Alternatively, press Ctrl+B to bold the text, Ctrl+U to underline the text, or Ctrl+I to italicize the text.)

3. To change the font, font size, or font color, choose Font from the submenu, and complete the dialog box shown in Figure 7.10. Choose OK to apply the changes.

F I G U R E   7.10   *Font Dialog Box*

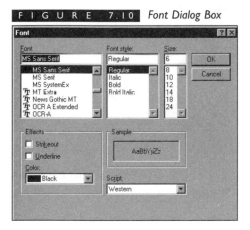

OLE Attachments

GroupWise 5's compatibility with industry standards, such as Object Linking and Embedding (OLE), makes it easy to share information among applications.

OLE is used to make an active "bridge" between different types of data (spreadsheet, database, document, and so on). This bridge is used to update all associated data types when one of them changes.

An extensive discussion of OLE is beyond the scope of this book, but we do want to show you how to add these objects to a GroupWise message. There are five operations you can use to add OLE objects to your messages:

- ► Edit,Links — Change the properties of the embedded object.
- ► Edit, Attach Object — Add an OLE object as a file attachment. Select the object and choose OK, as shown in Figure 7.11.
- ► Edit,Insert Object — Add an object into the body of the message. Select the object and choose OK, also shown in Figure 7.11.
- ► Edit,Object — Open the embedded object in the open GroupWise view.
- ► Edit,Convert to Static — Remove the updating quality of the embedded object.

FIGURE 7.11 *Insert/Attach an OLE Object*

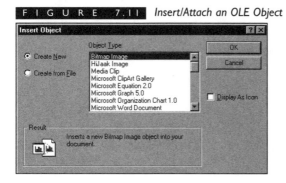

To embed a Word document into a GroupWise attachment (so the recipient can double-click on the attachment to open the application, instead of just viewing the file):

1. From a new message screen, choose OLE from the Edit menu. Choose Attach Object.

2. Make sure that Create New is selected and choose Microsoft Word Document from the list of object types. Click on OK.

3. Microsoft Word will launch, and the new, open document will be created as an attachment to the GroupWise message.

4. Make the necessary additions to the document and choose Update from the File menu to update the attachment with the final version of the new document. Choose Exit from the File menu when you are finished with the document.

5. From the new GroupWise message window, click on the Send button to send the document out.

6. The recipient can open the message as normal and will launch Microsoft Word with the file you created.

Summary

In this chapter, you saw how the powerful advanced features in GroupWise can help you be more productive. Mastering sending options, rules, discussions, and the other advanced topics we covered will set you apart as a true GroupWise guru.

CHAPTER 8

Document
Management

Document management is very different from file management. In file management, you store your files in directories and subdirectories on your hard drive (or on a network drive). In *document management,* all documents are stored in a central location on a network. Instead of storing your files in directories and subdirectories, your documents are stored in a database system.

The document management capabilities built into GroupWise 5 make it a unique product in the e-mail and groupware industry. GroupWise *document management services* (or *DMS*) is a feature that enables you to manage your documents in your GroupWise system. By integrating messaging and document management, GroupWise makes it easy to access and share documents with others.

You can use GroupWise document management features to:

▶ Store document files in the GroupWise system

▶ Access common files shared by members of your organization, company, or department and share your files with other users

▶ Maintain multiple versions of documents

▶ Search for documents stored in the system

NOTE   DMS must be configured at the GroupWise system level before individual users can utilize document management features. If you are unsure about whether document management is available at your organization, ask your system administrator.

Document Libraries

Document libraries are the heart of GroupWise document management systems. A *library* is a document storage location in a GroupWise system. Each library is set up by the system administrator. GroupWise users store documents in libraries and access shared documents that are stored there.

A GroupWise library is similar to a real-world public library. If you need a particular book, you can quickly find out if it is at the library by checking the card catalog system. You can locate a particular book by its author, title, or subject matter. Instead of books, GroupWise libraries store documents. You can find a document in a GroupWise library by running a search based on its title, author, or subject, as well as a number of other criteria collectively known as *document properties.*

Accessing Libraries

The system administrator sets up each library and determines library access privileges. For example, the administrator may set up a library that contains documents that everyone in the company needs to access, such as product marketing documents and expense report forms. The administrator may decide to only grant View rights so everyone can read the documents, but nobody else can change them. If your personal documents will be stored in the library, the administrator will need to grant you different access rights for those documents. To manage your personal documents in a library, you need to be able to view, create, modify, and delete them.

If you have questions about what you can or cannot do within a library in your system, ask your administrator.

Using Library Documents

Once a document is placed into a library, it can only be accessed through GroupWise or through an application that uses GroupWise document management services (called an *integrated application*).

NOTE Many Windows 95 applications, such as WordPerfect 7.0 and Microsoft Word for Windows 95, support GroupWise document management.

If you need to work on a document when you are not logged into GroupWise, you must first "check out" the document from the library and place it in a directory or on a disk. When you are finished working on the document, you check it back into the library. We explain how to check out and check in documents later in this chapter.

Documents stored in the library can be accessed in two ways: through document references in your GroupWise Mailboxes or through document searches. A *document reference* is an icon in your Mailbox, similar to a Mail message icon. Both methods are explained later in this chapter.

Setting a Default Library

A *default library* is the library where you store your documents by default. Although you may have access to many GroupWise libraries, you should specify one library as your default library.

To set a default library:

1. Click on Tools.

2. Click on Options.
3. Double-click on the Documents icon. The dialog box shown in Figure 8.1 appears.
4. Highlight the library you want as your default library, and click on the Set Default button.
5. Click on OK to save your settings, then click on Close to exit Options.

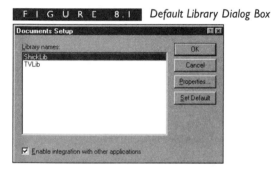

FIGURE 8.1 *Default Library Dialog Box*

IMPORTANT

All libraries to which you have been granted the View right will appear in the list when you double-click on the Documents icon. However, if you plan to store personal documents in your default library, you will need more than just the View right. Your system administrator can tell you which libraries are suitable for storing personal documents.

After you designate a default library, you can perform all of the document management functions that are enabled by your rights assignments. Of course, before you can do anything with library documents, the documents must first be placed in the library. You place documents in a library by either importing them or by creating them in the library.

Importing Documents into a Library

There are two methods for importing documents into a library: Quick Import and Custom Import.

IMPORTANT

Once a document is moved into a library, it can only be accessed through GroupWise or applications that integrate with GroupWise document management services. For example, if you create a document using Microsoft Word and save it in the library, you can still work on the document, but you use the GroupWise document management dialog boxes to retrieve the document in Word. You can choose to copy documents into the library and maintain a copy outside of the library, but you must then decide how both versions will be kept current.

Using Quick Import

Quick Import copies your documents into the default library with the default document property settings. (Document properties are explained later in this chapter.) Quick Import does not let you customize documents individually. Use a Quick Import when you need to place many files into the library all at once and you are not concerned about customizing the document properties for each document.

To perform a Quick Import:

1. Click on File.

2. Click on Import Documents. The dialog box shown in Figure 8.2 appears. Notice that the Quick Import option is selected by default.

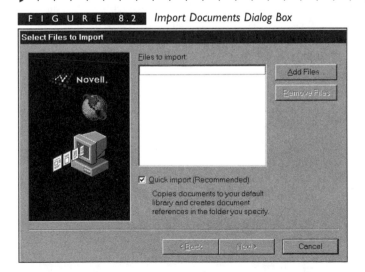

F I G U R E   8.2 *Import Documents Dialog Box*

3. Click on the Add Files button. A standard Windows 95 file dialog box appears.

4. Navigate to the desired directory, highlight the files you want to import, and click on OK. Repeat this step to add files from other directories.

5. Click on Next when all files are listed in the Import dialog box. The Create Document References dialog box appears, as shown in Figure 8.3.

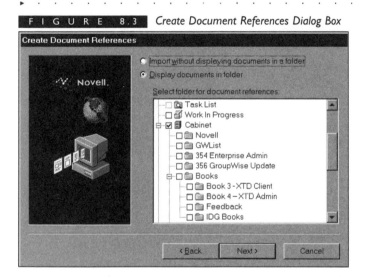

FIGURE 8.3 *Create Document References Dialog Box*

6. Choose the "Import without displaying documents in a folder" option to import the documents into the library without creating document references in your Mailbox, or

7. Choose the "Display documents in a folder" option to create document references in a folder you specify.

8. If you chose to display the documents in a folder, click on a check box in the Select Folder window to designate where the document references will appear. (Note: If you don't select a folder, a document reference will not be created.)

9. Click on Finish to perform the import. An import progress dialog box will appear, showing you the status of the import, and if any of the documents have failed to import correctly.

Quick Import *copies* documents into the library and leaves the files in your directory structure unchanged.

IMPORTANT

Using Custom Import

Custom Import gives you much more control over importing documents into the library. Custom Import enables you to:

- Specify which library you will import the documents into
- Specify document properties on a per-document basis
- Move or Copy documents into the library

To import documents using Custom Import:

1. Click on File.

2. Click on Import Documents.

3. Clear the Quick Import option by clicking on the check box.

4. Click on Add Files. A standard Windows 95 file dialog box appears.

5. Navigate to the desired directory, highlight the files you want to import, and click on OK. Repeat this step to add files from other directories.

6. Click on Next. The Import Method dialog box appears.

7. Choose between the Copy Documents and Move Documents options.

The Move option removes the files from your directories and places them in the library. Be sure you don't accidentally move operating system or application files into the library.

IMPORTANT

8. (Optional) If you want a log file, select the "Store all status and error messages into a log file" option, and specify a path and filename for the log file.

9. Choose Next. The Select Library dialog box appears.

10. Select the library into which the files will be imported, and choose Next. The Create Document References dialog box appears.

11. Choose the "Import without displaying documents in a folder" option to import the documents into the library without creating document references in your Mailbox, or

12. Choose the "Display documents in a folder" option to create document references in a folder you specify.

13. If you chose to display the documents in a folder, click a check box in the Select Folder window to designate where the document references appear.

14. Choose Next. The Set Document Property Options dialog box appears, as shown in Figure 8.4.

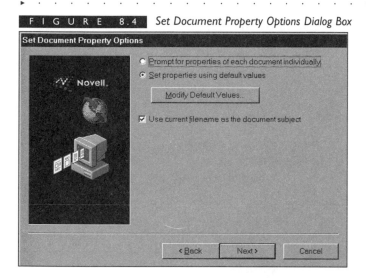

FIGURE 8.4 *Set Document Property Options Dialog Box*

15. Choose the "Prompt for properties of each document individually" option if you want to set different document properties for each document you chose in step 5. (This could be time consuming if you are importing many documents.) Alternatively,

16. Choose the "Set properties using default values" option to use the default properties for all documents.

17. (Optional) Use the Modify Default Values button to establish default document properties for the files being imported.

18. If you don't want the document filename to be the document subject line for the documents, clear the "Use current filename as the document subject" check box. (If you clear the check box, you are prompted to enter a subject for each document individually. Again, this could be tedious if you are importing many documents.)

19. Click on Next. The Import Document dialog box appears.

20. Click on Finish to start the import process.

After the import finishes, document references will appear in the folder you selected (assuming you chose the Create Reference option) and your documents will be available from the library. Remember, these documents cannot be accessed by others because you have not set up sharing properties. Also, remember that you must be running GroupWise to access the documents in the library.

Creating New Documents

In addition to importing existing documents into a GroupWise library, you can create new documents in a library.

To create a new document:

1. From the main GroupWise screen, click on File.

2. Click on New.

3. Click on Document. The New Document dialog box appears, as shown in Figure 8.5. When you create a new document, GroupWise prompts you to select a method for creating the document. You can select an application, a template, or a file. These options are explained in Table 8.1.

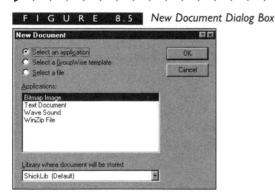

FIGURE 8.5 *New Document Dialog Box*

4. If you used a specific application to create the document, select the application and choose OK. Alternatively, if you want to base the document on a template, select the template and choose OK. If instead you want to base the document on a file, select the file and choose OK. The New Document dialog box appears, prompting you to enter a subject for the document.

WiseGuide

If you are opening an application that does not support GroupWise DMS, you will get a warning stating that you are opening a non-integrated application. Choose OK to bypass the warning. If you don't want to see the warning again, click the "Don't show this message again" check box. You can use non-integrated applications with GroupWise DMS; simply don't change the filename that is assigned by GroupWise while the document is open.

5. Enter a subject.

6. If you want to open the document, verify that the Open Document Now check box is selected, and choose OK. GroupWise will open the application that is associated with the document type, the application, or the file extension, depending upon the creation method you selected. For example, if the file extension is .DOC, GroupWise will launch Microsoft Word.

7. Create the document using the application.

8. Save the document using the assigned file-name.

9. Close the application.

The document will be saved in the GroupWise library.

TABLE 8.1 *Options for Creating a New Document*

OPTION	FUNCTION
Select an Application	You can select an application to create a document based on that application. The Applications list box shows all the applications that are registered in the Windows registry.
Select a Template	A template is a file you use to create other documents, such as a word processing document pre-formatted with the company letterhead, or a spreadsheet file that is set up to calculate an expense report.
	You can select GroupWise templates to use a document in the library as the foundation of a new document.
	If you have documents that you often use as a basis for creating new documents, you can add them to the library and assign them the document type "template." These templates will then appear in the templates list.
Select a File	You can select a file anywhere on your system and use it as a foundation for a new document.

Creating Document References

> **WiseGuide**
>
> If a document already exists in the library and you just want to create a document reference for it in your Mailbox, click on File, New, and Document Reference. You can also create a document reference by using the GroupWise Find feature to locate a document and drag the document to your Mailbox or folder.

When you create or import a document into the library, you have the option to create a *document reference* within a GroupWise folder. A document reference is similar to the icons you see in the Mailbox when you receive a Mail message. It is a pointer you use to access the document in the library.

Figure 8.6 shows a Mailbox that contains several document references. Notice that the icons resemble the applications that created the documents.

A document reference can exist in the same folders as GroupWise Mail messages, or you can create folders in your Mailbox for your documents (just like you would create directories in a file system).

F I G U R E 8.6 *Document References in the Mailbox*

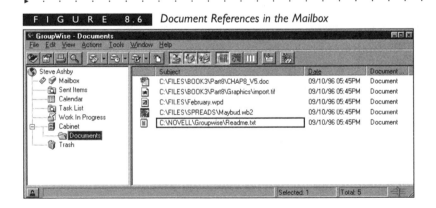

Checking Out Documents

When you open a document from the library, the document is marked as "In Use" and cannot be opened and modified by other users. However, there may be times when you want to work on the document while you are not running GroupWise. For example, you may need to modify the document while at home or while on a business trip. In this situation, you would need to "check out" the document.

When you check out a document, the document is marked as "In Use" until you check it back in. The document cannot be modified by other users; however, the document can be viewed by GroupWise users who have View rights.

You have two options when checking out documents:

▶ Check-Out Only

▶ Check-Out and Copy

If you choose the Check-Out Only option, the document is marked as Checked-out in the library and cannot be modified by others, but it is not copied to a directory for you to access it.

If you choose the Check-Out and Copy option, the document is copied to the directory you specify.

To check out a document:

WiseGuide

To find out who has a document checked out of the library:

1. Right-click on the document reference.
2. Choose Properties.
3. Select the Activity Log tab.

1. Highlight the document reference in your Mailbox.

2. Click on Actions and then on Check-Out. The dialog box shown in Figure 8.7 appears.

3. Type a filename for the document in the Checked-Out Filename field. (By default, GroupWise uses the document number as the check-out filename. You can specify a different filename.)

4. Enter a path for the document in the Checked-Out Location field.

5. Click on the Check-Out button.

FIGURE 8.7 *Check-Out Dialog Box*

Once you have checked out a document, you can open it from the directory and change it while you are not running GroupWise. The changes you make do not appear in the document in the library until you check it back in or update it.

Checking In Documents

After you are finished with a document that you have checked out from a library, you must check the document back in so any changes are reflected in the library. Checking in a document unlocks the document so it can be modified by other users.

WiseGuide

You can check in multiple documents at once by holding Ctrl and clicking on multiple documents in the Documents to be Checked-In dialog box.

To check in a document:

1. Highlight the document reference in your Mailbox.

2. Click on Actions and then on Check-In. The dialog box shown in Figure 8.8 appears.

3. Choose the Check-in method.

FIGURE 8.8 *Check-In Dialog Box*

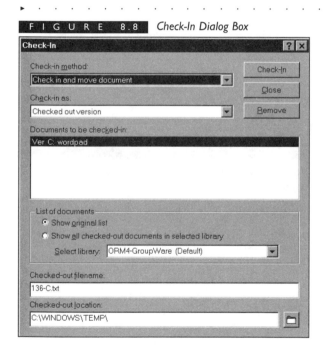

You have four options for checking in documents, as shown in Table 8.2.

TABLE 8.2	*Check-In Method Options*
OPTION	**EXPLANATION**
Check-In and Move	Moves the document to the library and deletes it from the check-out location
Check-In and Copy	Copies the document to the library and leaves a copy in the check-out location
Check-In Only	Checks the document back in to the library, but does not update the document in the library with any changes you made to the checked-out version
Update Without Checking-In	Updates the document in the library with the changes you have made, but does not unlock the document

When you check in a document, you also have three options that relate to document versions, as shown in Table 8.3.

TABLE 8.3	*Check-In Version Options*
OPTION	**EXPLANATION**
Checked-out version	Keeps the same document version as the version you checked out
New version	Enables you to specify a new document version
New Document	Enables you to create an entirely new document in the library and specify new document properties

Remember that if you are updating documents and you will be connected to the GroupWise system, you do not have to go through the check-out, check-in process. When you open a document in the library, it is marked as In Use until you close the document. Other users cannot open and modify the document while you have it open. You only need to check out a document when you will be working on it while not connected to GroupWise.

Copying Documents

Use the document copy feature to create a document identical to one in the library and make changes without altering the original.

When you copy a document, you need to specify the new document's properties. You can manually specify the properties, or you can use the properties of the source document.

To copy a document:

1. Highlight one or more document references in your Mailbox.

2. Click on Actions and then on Copy Document. The Copy Document dialog box appears, as shown in Figure 8.9.

3. Choose the library where the document will be copied to from the drop-down list.

4. Specify the method for creating the properties for the new document(s).

5. Click on OK.

New document references appear in your Mailbox.

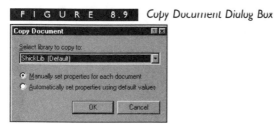

FIGURE 8.9 *Copy Document Dialog Box*

Deleting Documents

If you have been given Delete rights, you can delete documents from the library.

You have three choices when deleting documents:

▶ Delete the document reference from your Mailbox. Only the document reference is removed and the document itself remains in the library.

▶ Delete the selected version of the document. The document reference is removed from your Mailbox and previous versions remain in the library.

▶ Delete all versions of the document. The document reference is removed from your Mailbox and all versions of the document are removed from the library.

GroupWise automatically deletes documents that have exceeded their defined document life, as specified in the document type definition. Each document type has an expiration date and expiration action (delete or archive). To delete a document:

1. Highlight the document reference in your Mailbox.

2. Click on Edit

3. Click on Delete. The dialog box shown in Figure 8.10 appears.

4. Choose the deletion method you want.

5. Click on OK.

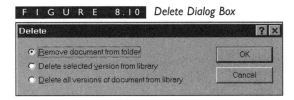

F I G U R E   8 . 1 0   *Delete Dialog Box*

Document Searches

One of the advantages of document management is that it makes finding documents extremely easy. Instead of hunting through directories and trying to recognize cryptic eight-character filenames, with GroupWise DMS, you can search for documents using a number of different criteria.

Document Properties

Every document in a GroupWise library has a set of attributes that uniquely identify the document, such as the author's name, the date the document was created, and the document type. These attributes are *document properties*. You use document properties to find documents that have been placed in a library.

You can set document properties when you import a document into the library or when you create the document. You can also edit the document properties through the document reference, by right-clicking on the reference and selecting the Properties option. The document properties dialog box is shown in Figure 8.11.

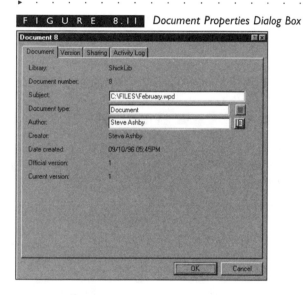

F I G U R E   8.11 *Document Properties Dialog Box*

As shown in Figure 8.11, there are four categories of document properties: Document, Version, Sharing, and Activity Log. The most common document properties and their descriptions are listed in Table 8.4.

TABLE 8.4 *Document Properties*

PROPERTY	DESCRIPTION
Library	The library that contains the document
Document Number	A number assigned by GroupWise that is used by the document management system to identify the document
Subject	A text field that enables you to assign a descriptive subject for the document, such as "1996 Annual Report"
	When you import documents, you have the option to make the filename and path the document subject. Otherwise, you can specify the subject as you create the document, or you can edit the subject in the properties dialog box.
Document Type	A classification for the document that is used to categorize and establish the usage of the document. For example, some common document types include: Agenda, Contract, Memo, Minutes, Proposal, and Report.
	These classifications, or types, facilitate searches for specific documents. An important field in Document Type is the expiration setting. The expiration setting determines when a document expires and what should be done with the document when it expires.
Author	The author of the document. The author is not always the same as the creator. The author can be any GroupWise user.
Creator	The person who placed the document in the library
Date Created	The date and time the document was placed in the library (Note: If you imported the document from a file system, the date and time stamp on the file is not preserved in the document properties.)
Current Version	GroupWise document management services allow up to 100 versions of a document. The current version is the latest version of the document.

(continued)

Official Version	The version of the document that will be identified and viewed through searches. For example, if seven versions of the annual report were stored in the library, and version 6 was designated as the official version, it would be the version found in searches by GroupWise users who have View rights to the library. (Version 7 could be a draft in progress that is not yet ready for official release.)
	Any version of a document can be identified as the official version. If you do not specify an official version, the current version is the official version. Usually the official version is designated by the creator of the document, but the right to set the official version can be granted to others.
Description	A text field that enables you to describe the current version of the document. By default, the description for the first version of a document will be "Original."
Status	The document statuses include:
	Available. The document is available to be opened or checked out of the library.
	In Use. Another user currently has the document opened or checked out.
	Checked-Out. Another user has checked out the document.
Sharing	Shows the GroupWise users with whom you have shared the documents. You control the sharing properties for the documents you add to the library. By default, a document is not shared and cannot be accessed by other users. Sharing documents is discussed later in this chapter. (Note: The rights you specify for shared documents apply to all versions of the document.)
Activity Log	The Activity Log property shows you a chronological log of the actions that have been performed on the document, such as who created the document, who has opened the document, who has viewed the document, and who has edited the document.

IMPORTANT

You must have the Edit right to the library to change a document's properties. You will likely have this right for your documents, but you may not have this right for public documents.

Setting Default Document Properties

You can set default properties that will be used for all documents you import or create. To set default document properties:

1. Click on Tools.

2. Click on Options.

3. Double-click on the Documents icon.

4. Change any properties contained in the dialog box.

5. Choose OK.

The values you set become the default properties for any documents you create or import in the library.

Using Find

In Chapter 4, we discussed how to use the Find feature. The Advanced Find options are very useful for searching document libraries.

NOTE

When you use the Find feature, GroupWise searches for your document in the default library first.

To find a document using Standard Find options:

1. Click on Actions.

2. Click on Find.

3. Type the word or words you want to find.

4. Select the Look In tab.

5. Select the Mailbox, the libraries, or both.

6. Click on OK.

GroupWise will perform the search and return a list of documents or messages that meet your specified search criteria.

> **WiseGuide**
>
> You can expand the Mailbox to select individual folders or the All Libraries icon to select individual libraries.

To find a document using Advanced Find options:

1. Click on Actions and then on Find.

2. Click on the Advanced Find button.

3. Specify the find criteria using the Advanced Find dialog box. Figure 8.12 shows how to find all entries where the author is Kellie Rogers, the library is the Corporate Library, and the subject contains the word "golf."

4. Click on OK to begin the search.

GroupWise presents you with a list of the documents that met the search criteria.

FIGURE 8.12 *Advanced Find*

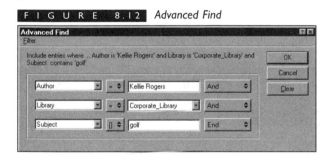

Document Sharing

When you place documents in a library, you control who has access to those documents through the Sharing tab of the document properties screen. You also control what rights others have to the document.

To share a document with other users:

1. Right-click on the document reference in your Mailbox and choose Properties.

2. Click on the Sharing tab. The dialog box shown in Figure 8.13 appears. The default sharing property is Not Shared. Not Shared means that no other GroupWise user has access to the document. Notice that GroupWise inserts <General User Access> and <Author/ Creator Access> in the Share list. By default, general users (all

users with access to the library) do not have any rights to the document and the author/creator has full rights to the document.

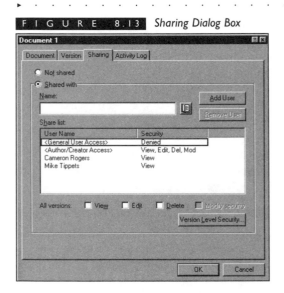

FIGURE 8.13 *Sharing Dialog Box*

3. Click on the Shared With option.

4. Type the user name in the Name: field and click on Add User. Alternatively, you can click the Address Book tab and double-click on the user's name in the address list. The user name appears in the Share List window.

By default, the new users have the View right, which means that the users can locate the document in searches and can view the document, but cannot modify it.

IMPORTANT

The rights you specify are for all versions of a document. If you want to specify different rights for each version of a document, click on the Version Level Security button.

To specify additional rights:

1. Highlight the user in the Share List window.
2. Click on the check boxes for Edit, Delete, or Modify Security to grant those rights. Table 8.5 lists the user rights options for a document.

TABLE 8.5	User Rights Options for a Document
RIGHT	**DESCRIPTION**
Edit	Users can make changes to the document.
Delete	Users can delete the document. Use this right with care.
Modify Security	Users can modify the rights for the document. If you grant this right, the users can modify the other rights, and could grant themselves the Edit and Delete rights.

Use the <General User Access> entry to grant the same rights to all users who have access to the library. For example, if for some reason you want everyone to be able to delete the file, highlight <General User Access> and grant the Delete right.

NOTE

A user must have the Edit right before he or she can have the Modify Security right.

> **WiseGuide**
>
> You can share document references with other users by sharing your folder that contains the document references. Sharing your folder requires that the recipient of the shared folder have rights to access the document in the library.

When you grant users Edit or Delete rights, GroupWise automatically gives them View rights to the document. Without the View right, a user cannot see the document in the results of a Find, in shared folders, and so on.

When you grant other users rights to the document, the users do not automatically receive a document reference in their Mailboxes. They can only access the document by using Find.

Summary

In this chapter we explained the basics of document management. The GroupWise online help system provides extensive information about document management and also includes a guide entitled "Managing Your Documents" to help you get started.

In the next chapter we explain how to use GroupWise Remote Mode to remain connected while you are away from the office.

CHAPTER 9

Remote Mode

With today's mobile workforce, access to e-mail and scheduling information is more critical than ever. If you can access your messaging system regardless of where you are, you can communicate with your customers and coworkers as if you were sitting in your office.

This chapter addresses how to configure the GroupWise client for remote access. We look at the steps necessary to access information when you're out of the office — how to request your messages and how to connect to the system and download your messages. We also explain the different techniques to use when you are connected to a network and when you are working off-line using a remote Mailbox.

Preparing to Use GroupWise in Remote Mode

Before we get into the actual mouse clicks and keystrokes needed to configure and use GroupWise in Remote Mode, there is some information gathering that you need to do. Your GroupWise system administrator needs to provide you with some information that GroupWise will ask you for: domain name, post office name, phone number of the Async gateway, login ID, and password.

You also need to find out how you are going to connect to the GroupWise system when you are not in the office. There are three types of connections possible:

- ▶ *Network*. Using a drive letter and path to your post office on a network, possibly achieved through a dial-in, network-connection software package such as NetWare Connect.

- ▶ *TCP/IP*. Using the TCP/IP address of the GroupWise Mail server that synchronizes your Master Mailbox with your Remote Mailbox.

- ▶ *Modem*. Using a dial-up connection to the GroupWise Async gateway that forwards your incoming and outgoing messages.

The next step in preparing to set up GroupWise Remote Mode is assigning a password to your Master Mailbox. You need to set a password on your Master Mailbox before GroupWise 5 Remote Mode will work. You must do this while you are logged into the network.

To set a password on your Master Mailbox:

1. Select Options from the Tools menu and double-click on the Security icon.

2. Type a password in the New Password field and in the Confirm New Password field. Choose OK to set the password. The next time you start GroupWise, you will need to type in your password.

(If you never log into the network, the system administrator can set a password on your Mailbox and tell you what it is.)

IMPORTANT

The password is case-sensitive. Also, be sure to record your password somewhere secure.

Finally, you need to install GroupWise 5 on the hard drive of the computer you will be using in Remote Mode. You should contact your system administrator to help you set this up. (If the computer you use at work is the same as the computer you use when working off-line in Remote Mode, simply make sure GroupWise is installed on the hard drive. The standard GroupWise client is all you need to run in Remote Mode.)

Configuring the GroupWise Client

If you start the GroupWise program while you are not connected to or logged into the network, choose "Connect to a remote database" from the dialog box that appears. You may then perform the procedures explained in this chapter.

The setup for GroupWise 5 is very intuitive, using a lot of information that has been built into Windows 95. For example, GroupWise 5 can detect the type of modem installed on your computer.

You need to obtain most of the other setup information from your GroupWise system administrator. Once you have this information, configuring GroupWise Remote is a matter of completing some simple steps. Once the configuration is complete, you most likely won't need to change the settings unless your master system changes or you change your connection method.

TIP

> It is a good idea to record your remote information, in case you need to re-enter it at a later date.

The first time you run GroupWise while not connected to the network, you will see the screen shown in Figure 9.1. This window displays a list of what needs to be set up so you can access your Remote Mailbox.

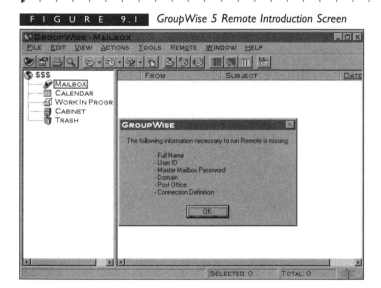

F I G U R E   9 . 1 *GroupWise 5 Remote Introduction Screen*

Once you click on OK, you see the Remote Options dialog box, as shown in Figure 9.2. (To change your remote configurations later, you can access this screen by choosing Tools, Options, and double-clicking on the Remote icon.)

The GroupWise 5 Remote Options can be categorized into four areas: User Information, System Information, Creating Connections, and Time Zone.

User Information

First, enter the user information, as shown in Figure 9.2.

User Information

Full Name

You must enter your complete name (first and last), which will help identify your messages.

> If you want the recipients of your messages to be able to tell
> when you have sent a message remotely, add (Remote) after
> your name. (Any text is valid on this line.)
TIP

User ID

This field requires your GroupWise User ID that was set up for you by the
system administrator. It is *not* case-sensitive, but spelling definitely counts!

Password

You must enter your Master Mailbox password in this field for remote access:

1. Click on the Password button next to Master Mailbox password.

2. Type in the password, and confirm it by retyping the password.

3. Click on OK.

This process completes the user information portion of setup.

System Information

Next, enter the system information, as shown in Figure 9.3.

GroupWise 5 System Information

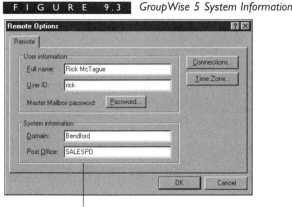

System Information

The information you enter in the fields for system information must be obtained from your system administrator. (Domains and post offices are logical divisions of your GroupWise system and are defined by the GroupWise system administrator.)

Domain

Type in the name of your GroupWise domain, provided to you by the system administrator.

Post Office

Type in the name of your GroupWise post office, provided to you by the system administrator.

This process completes the system information part of setup.

Creating Connections

From the Remote Options screen, click on the Connections button to create connections to the master system. You will see the Connection Configuration dialog box shown in Figure 9.4.

You must create at least one connection before you can start using GroupWise 5 Remote.

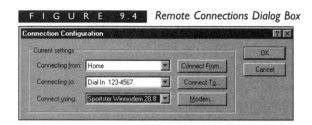

FIGURE 9.4 *Remote Connections Dialog Box*

If you want to return to this point later on (for example, to add, change, or delete connections), choose the Send/Retrieve option from the Remote menu and click on the Configure button.

Connecting From

The Connecting from: field in the Connection Configuration dialog box is where you can create multiple remote *profiles*. For example, you can create a profile for getting remote messages from home or on the road (complete with a 9 before the area code and phone number).

Figure 9.5 shows the dialog box for creating a "dialing from" location. Select your location from the "I am dialing from" drop-down list, verify the location, and choose OK.

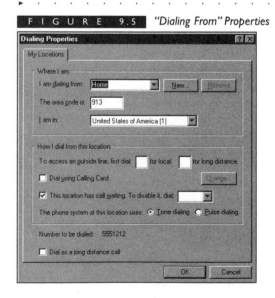

FIGURE 9.5 *"Dialing From" Properties*

Connecting To (Modem, Network, and TCP/IP)

In order to send and receive information while you are not connected to the network, you need to create a *remote connection*. Later, when you select the Connecting to: field in the Connection Configuration dialog box, you will be able to create, modify, or delete your connections, as shown in Figure 9.6.

FIGURE 9.6 *Connections Listing and Selection Screen*

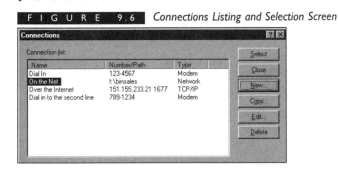

The connection you define determines how your computer will communicate with the GroupWise system. You can create as many connections as there are available in your GroupWise system. (Your system administrator will have connection information for you.) Some of the fields you complete might not make sense to you, but they are necessary to protect the security of the GroupWise system.

To create a new connection, click on the New button from the Connections screen. As Figure 9.7 shows, there are three types of remote connections: Modem, Network, and TCP/IP. We will discuss only the modem connection here, because the modem is by far the most common type of remote connection. We explain Network and TCP/IP connections at the end of this chapter.

FIGURE 9.7 *New Connections Screen*

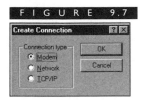

A *modem connection* is used to dial into the GroupWise Async gateway. The settings for this connection are determined by your system administrator. Figure 9.8 shows the Modem Connection dialog box.

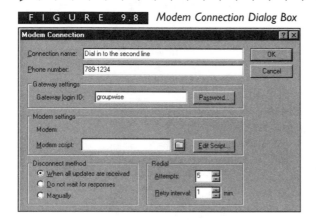

FIGURE 9.8 *Modem Connection Dialog Box*

To create a modem connection:

1. Choose Modem from the Connections screen.

2. Enter a name for the connection in the Connection name: field, and enter the phone number in the Phone number: field.

NOTE   You won't need to include extra numbers to obtain an outside or long distance line if you have created a "Connecting From" profile for your location. See "Connecting From" earlier in this chapter for more information.

3. The Gateway settings area is where you will enter information needed to connect to the GroupWise Asynchronous gateway (a techy name for the computer that answers the phone when your computer calls in for messages). Enter the Gateway login ID, and click on the Password button to enter the gateway's password. You will need to retype the password. (Remember, all passwords in GroupWise are case-sensitive.)

4. Enter the redial information (the number of attempts and how long to wait in between each attempt) — the defaults are usually sufficient.

5. Choose a disconnect method and then choose OK to save the connection. The connection options all have one area in common: the disconnect method.

When all updates are received keeps the connection open until all responses have been received.

Do not wait for responses forces the disconnection as soon as requests are uploaded. You will see your responses the next time you connect.

Manually keeps the connection open until you click on the Disconnect button.

Connect Using (Modem Selection)

The "Connect using:" portion of the Connection Configuration dialog box tells GroupWise Remote what device you will connect to the GroupWise system with. From this screen, you see a list of all available ports.

As you can see from Figure 9.9, all of the hardware ports installed in your computer will appear. Also notice that your installed modem in Windows 95 appears on the list; GroupWise Remote will use this modem.

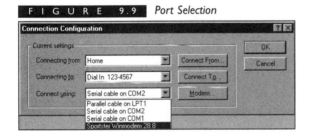

FIGURE 9.9 *Port Selection*

If you would like to configure the modem, click on the Modem button. Notice that you can change the general modem properties, the connection preferences (only for the modem, not for GroupWise connections), and other dialing options, as shown in Figure 9.10.

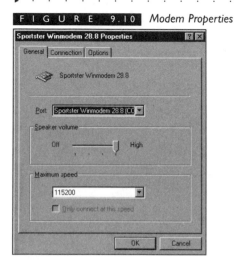

F I G U R E   9.10   *Modem Properties*

Any alterations you make here will change the modem's properties in Windows 95, not just in GroupWise. The GroupWise program gives you a convenient way of accessing the modem setup through the program, instead of using Control Panel.

Once the three Connection Configuration settings have been specified — Connecting from:, Connecting to:, and Connect using: — choose OK and the connection information will be saved in your Connections List. You are now ready to complete the last area of GroupWise Remote configuration, the Time Zone.

Time Zone

GroupWise needs to know the time zone where you reside so it can automatically adjust appointment times. This setting is important if you live in a time zone different than the time zone where your master GroupWise system is located.

To set your time zone, click on the Time Zone button and choose the appropriate time zone from the list. As Figure 9.11 shows, the time zone for your computer is displayed graphically.

Setting the Time Zone

Like your modem selection, the Time Zone setting should be automatically set by Windows 95.

Using GroupWise in Remote Mode

There are very few functional differences between using GroupWise Remote and using GroupWise while logged into the network. The same set of program files are used, the screens all look the same, and you access all of your information the same way.

When you use GroupWise in the office ("connected" mode), you are working in your Master Mailbox, which is stored on the network. When you leave the office and need to use GroupWise, the program will use a remote version of your Mailbox, stored on your computer at home, or perhaps your notebook computer. The messages and Calendar items you create in the Remote Mode are stored in the Remote Mailbox until you connect to the GroupWise system and synchronize the two Mailboxes.

Remember to connect after the last change you make to your Remote Mailbox. Otherwise, the master system will not be informed of the changes.

Remote Menu

One of the most noticeable differences about Remote Mode is a new menu, aptly called Remote.

As you can see in Figure 9.12, there are four choices under the Remote menu:

- *Send/Retrieve.* Configure and initiate the remote connection here.

- *Retrieve Selected Items.* Retrieve the remaining portions of incomplete messages (because of item-request restrictions, such as when you retrieve subject lines only).

- *Pending Requests.* View and manage requests that are waiting to be uploaded and responded to by the master system. Usually, you won't need to do anything in this screen.

- *Connection Log.* View the connection details in the log file. You can also see this information if you click on the Show Log button when you make a connection to the master system.

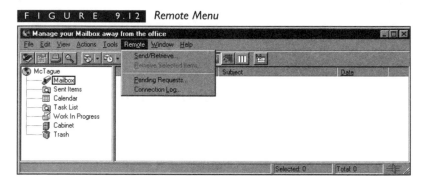

FIGURE 9.12 *Remote Menu*

There is also a Remote icon added to the Options choice under the Tools menu where you can change your Remote configuration. See "Configuring the GroupWise Client" section earlier in this chapter.

Sending Messages

For the most part, there is not much difference between using GroupWise remotely and using it on the network: You send messages, create Calendar entries, and reply to and forward messages the same way. The only difference is that you need to connect to the master system to actually send messages. See the section called "Connecting to the Master System" later in this chapter.

Busy Search

Busy Search is slightly different if you are in Remote Mode. When you are creating an Appointment while you are out of the office, you may not want to wait until the Appointment request has been received (and either accepted or declined) by the people you need at the meeting. If you need faster information about whether they are available for an Appointment or not, set up Busy Search in the normal way. (See Chapter 6 for a complete discussion of Busy Search on the network).

Once you have configured the Appointment information for the Busy Search, choose to connect now or wait until the next time you connect to send the Busy Search request to the GroupWise system, as shown in Figure 9.13. Either way, you will receive the results of your Busy Search, and you can continue creating your Appointment request.

FIGURE 9.13 *Remote Busy Search Screen*

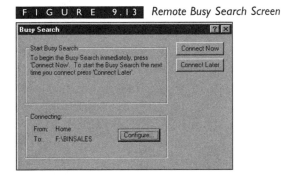

NOTE   You should save the incomplete Appointment in the "Work In Progress" folder while you are waiting for the outcome of the Busy Search. When the results arrive, open the draft Appointment, complete the information, and choose Send. Don't forget to connect again to actually send the message to the system.

Proxy

The only feature you cannot utilize when you are using GroupWise Remote is the Proxy feature. Since the Proxy feature involves having access to someone else's Mailbox (and you are not logged into the network where the other user's Mailbox is), there is no way to use this feature.

Connecting to the Master System

GroupWise Remote Mode is a *request-based system*. A request-based system means that you work off-line reading messages, creating new Appointments, and making other changes to your Remote Mailbox. Once you have made all of your changes and are ready to connect to the main system, you will generate a list of requests for items.

One request will be to send out all of your outgoing messages. Another request will be to retrieve your new messages, sent to you since the last time you connected to the main GroupWise system. You can make other requests (for example, to get a new copy of the Address Book). When you connect using any of the methods listed in the previous section, your requests are transferred to the main GroupWise system.

The GroupWise system will generate responses to your requests, compress them, and transfer them via your connection to your Remote computer. Some of your requests will be handled in the same session that you sent them in (to get your new messages, for example), and others will be transferred the next time you connect.

Once the request list has been completed, the connection is terminated, and the responses are decompressed and added to your Remote Mailbox.

To request items:

1. Choose Send/Retrieve from the Tools menu. The screen shown in Figure 9.14 appears.

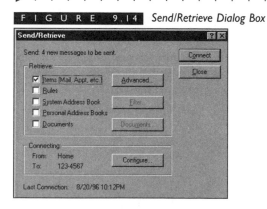

FIGURE 9.14 *Send/Retrieve Dialog Box*

2. If you would like to change the request for items, click on the Advanced button to display the screen shown in Figure 9.15. Choose the options you want from the tabs:

FIGURE 9.15
Configuring the Request for Items

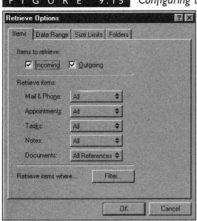

- *Items* enables you to select what message categories you want to update (Mail & Phone, Appointments, and so on) and set up a filter to retrieve specific messages matching certain criteria, for example, messages that contain "Miller Project" in the subject. See Chapter 4 for a complete discussion of using filters.

- *Date Range* enables you to set the range of dates from which GroupWise will retrieve messages. The default is five days prior to the current day. If you have not connected in several days, you may need to increase this range.

- *Size Limits* will retrieve messages that fall into a particular size range. (For example, you can only retrieve messages with attachments that are less than 30K in size.) You can also retrieve just the subject line, and then get the message information later. This feature can be very useful to minimize connection time and phone charges.

TIP
If after reading messages in the Mailbox, you decide you need to see the complete message or attachment, choose Retrieve Selected Items from the Tools menu and connect in the normal way. The balance of the message content will be downloaded. You can use Ctrl-click to select more than one message, in order to save connection time.

▸ *Folders* enables you to select the folders you want updated. You can use this feature in conjunction with the Rules feature to move only those messages you want retrieved to a certain Remote folder, so you can simply download messages from this folder. The Folder feature makes the Remote connection more efficient. Simply click on the box next to the folder to select it for updating.

3. Click on OK to return to the Send/Retrieve screen.

4. Make other selections from the Send/Retrieve screen as desired:

   ▸ *Rules* will update all Rules between the Remote and Master Mailboxes.

   ▸ *System Address Book* will update your Remote Mailbox with the most current Address Book. Click on Filter to select which address book you want (your Post Office or Domain).

   ▸ *Personal Address Book* will synchronize your Master and Remote personal address books.

   ▸ *Documents* will enable you to select the documents you want to retrieve if you have GroupWise Document Management Services enabled on your system. You can select documents from their folders, and the documents will be transferred to your Mailbox. See Chapter 8 for more information about document management.

5. Verify that the connection you want to use appears at the bottom of the screen. If you need to change the connection, click on the Configure button and set up the desired connection. See "Creating Connections" earlier in this chapter for more information.

6. Choose Connect to complete the request and connect to the master system.

The Connection Status screen appears, as shown in Figure 9.16.

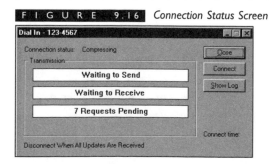

F I G U R E   9 . 1 6   *Connection Status Screen*

To see the details of the connection, click on the Show Log button. The Connection Log, shown in Figure 9.17, displays the session information and can be helpful in troubleshooting. This information is saved in a log file and can be accessed from the Connection Log option under the Tools menu.

Connection Log

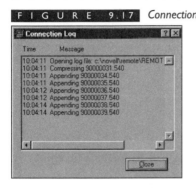

 NOTE It is a good idea to leave the computer alone while the connection is taking place. Any additional activity could slow the connection process or disrupt the link. During the connection activities, your computer is processing the new messages it just received, and you will see the dialog box shown in Figure 9.18.

Updating Remote Mailbox

Network and TCP/IP Connections

A *network connection* enables you to directly connect with your main GroupWise system through the network. This connection is used most often by people who travel to a branch office with a wide area network (WAN) link to the network.

All you need to know to use a network connection is the proper drive letter and a path to your GroupWise post office, as shown in Figure 9.19. Your system administrator should be able to provide you with this information.

FIGURE 9.19 *Network Connection Dialog Box*

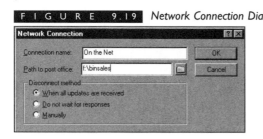

To create a network connection:

1. Choose Network from the Create Connection dialog box (shown in Figure 9.7).

2. In the Network Connection dialog box, enter a name for the connection in the Connection name: field.

3. In the Path to post office: field, enter the drive letter and path to your post office.

4. Choose a disconnect method and then OK to save the connection.

A *TCP/IP connection* is very similar to the network connection. Instead of specifying the drive letter and path to your GroupWise post office, you specify the TCP/IP address of the post office server. Again, your system administrator can give you this information.

TCP/IP stands for *Transmission Control Protocol/Internet Protocol.* Basically, TCP/IP is a networking language that computers use to communicate. The Internet uses this protocol. A TCP/IP connection requires that the TCP/IP protocol be set up on your computer. In Windows 95, you can find out if TCP/IP is set up by following these steps:

1. From the Start button, choose Settings and Control Panel.

2. Double-click on the Network icon.

3. Scroll down the list of items until you see "TCP/IP --> NE2000" (instead of NE2000, you may see the name of your particular brand of network card, or you may see the words "Dial Up Adapter").

IMPORTANT

Don't change any of the settings in this or any other network screen unless your system administrator instructs you to do so.

If you don't have an entry for the TCP/IP protocol, you will need to add that protocol to your system to use a TCP/IP connection. (See your Windows 95 manual for instructions on how to do this, or contact your system administrator.)

To create a TCP/IP connection to your GroupWise post office:

1. Choose the TCP/IP button from the New Connection dialog box. The dialog box shown in Figure 9.20 appears.

2. Type in a name for the connection in the Connection name: field.

3. Enter the IP address of the post office server in the IP Address: field. (The address will be four numbers that are up to three digits each, separated by periods. See the example in Figure 9.20.)

4. Enter the port number in the IP Port: field. This number is usually 1677, but you can confirm this with your system administrator.

5. Choose a disconnect method and then OK to save the connection.

F I G U R E   9 . 2 0   *TCP/IP Connection Dialog Box*

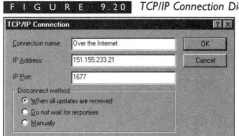

Hit the Road

One of the easiest features of GroupWise is also probably the most useful feature for Remote users. *Hit the Road* is a one-step way to update your Remote Mailbox before you leave the office.

As one of the preparations for your road trip, use the Hit the Road feature to do a last-minute synchronization of your Remote Mailbox and you are ready to go.

To use Hit the Road:

1. While logged into GroupWise, finish all messaging transactions (replies, new messages, and so on).

2. Choose Hit the Road from the Tools menu. The dialog box shown in Figure 9.21 appears.

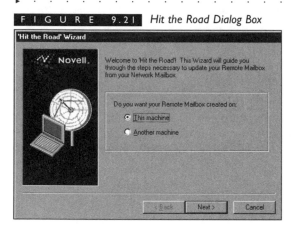

FIGURE 9.21 *Hit the Road Dialog Box*

NOTE

You may see a message about needing to set a password on your Mailbox before you can use Hit the Road. The Security Options screen will appear. Enter a password (case-sensitive), confirm it on the second line, and choose OK.

3. If a Remote Mailbox has never been created on this machine, you will be walked through setting it up on either this or another computer. If a Remote Mailbox has been set up previously, skip to step 6.

4. Choose "This machine" and click on Next. (If you choose "Another machine," you can copy the setup file to a floppy disk. This choice should only be made by the system administrator.)

5. Enter the path to the Remote Mailbox. (Your system administrator may have a desired location, but you can choose anywhere you like on your C drive.) The default is C:\NOVELL\REMOTE. Click on Next to move to the next screen.

6. Select which items you want to be updated to your Remote Mailbox *this time* by Hit the Road. You can configure the items each time you use Hit the Road, as shown in Figure 9.22.

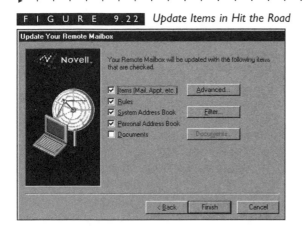

F I G U R E   9.22 *Update Items in Hit the Road*

If you would like to customize your items choices, click on the Advanced button and make the appropriate selections.

NOTE

7. You can choose which address book you need to use by clicking on the Filter button next to the System Address Book item. Select any of the items in the list to limit your Address Book as you like, as shown in Figure 9.23. (Chapter 4 includes a more complete discussion of the Filter box.)

8. If GroupWise Document Management is set up on your system, you can also select the documents you need by clicking on the box next to Documents. You can then select the documents you need by clicking on the Documents button and making your selection.

9. Choose Finish. This action will initiate a network connection to your post office, and the items you selected will be downloaded into your Remote Mailbox.

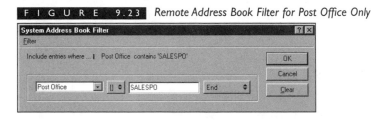

F I G U R E   9.23 *Remote Address Book Filter for Post Office Only*

Congratulations! You are now ready to Hit the Road.

IMPORTANT

You will see two or three extra windows open and close automatically while the synchronization takes place. If you want more information about what is happening, click on the Show Log button of the Network Connection screen. While the update takes place, it is important to leave the mouse alone! Just let the process finish, and as long as there are no extra windows open that show connection activities, you can use the system.

Smart Docking

Suppose you are using a notebook computer and have been away on a business trip. When you come back into the office after using GroupWise Remote, any changes you have made while on the road since your last connection can be automatically updated to the network's master version of your Mailbox (your Master Mailbox). This feature is known as *Smart Docking*.

When you start GroupWise the first time after being off of the network, GroupWise automatically synchronizes the changes in your Remote Mailbox with your Master Mailbox. Because the connection type — modem or logged into the network — is sensed automatically, no configuration is necessary. The dialog box in Figure 9.24 displays what you will see.

F I G U R E   9.24 *Remote Update Dialog Box*

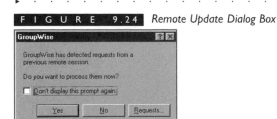

NOTE

If you select the "Don't display this prompt again" message, the message will update without any user intervention.

The update box is very similar to the other Network Connection screen in GroupWise Remote, as shown in Figure 9.25.

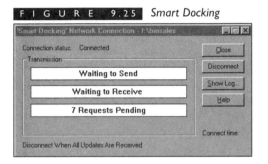

F I G U R E   9 . 2 5   *Smart Docking*

With the Smart Docking feature of GroupWise, you don't need to worry about how you are connected to GroupWise.

Summary

GroupWise Remote enables mobile users to take their information with them, access it while they're gone, and update the GroupWise system when they get back. The ability to stay in touch with critical communications can make a big difference in today's fast-paced world.

CHAPTER 10

Customizing
GroupWise

GroupWise enables you to customize your environment to reflect your own personal work style and preferences. In this chapter we'll explain the options for customizing your GroupWise environment.

Often, you can select options to override the defaults you set. For example, you may decide to set your default message priority level to Normal. When you need to send a high-priority message, you can change the priority level to High for that particular message (without changing the default). The next message you create will again use the default, Normal priority level, unless you decide to override the default again.

In this chapter, we explain how to set GroupWise default options, how to customize the Toolbar, and how to customize your folders.

Setting Default Options

When you click on Tools and then Options from the main GroupWise menu, you see the dialog box shown in Figure 10.1. Use this dialog box to set your GroupWise default options (in other words, your preferences).

F I G U R E   10.1 *GroupWise Options Dialog Box*

You can set defaults for the GroupWise environment (that is, the overall program interface), for sending messages, for document management, for security, and for the Calendar.

NOTE

The default settings for document management (the settings that correspond to the Document icon in the Options dialog box) are explained in Chapter 8.

Environment

The Environment preferences group enables you to modify characteristics of the overall GroupWise program interface. When you double-click on the Environment icon, you see a dialog box with five different tabs: General, Views, File Location, Cleanup, and Signature, as shown in Figure 10.2.

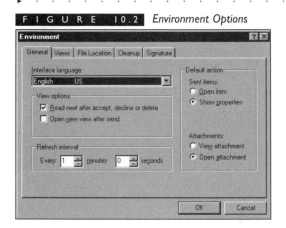

F I G U R E   1 0 . 2 *Environment Options*

General

Under the General tab, you can set the following preferences:

- ▶ *Interface language.* The language you want to use in the client interface (menus, views, and so on). If the language you desire does not appear, contact your system administrator. Languages are enabled at the system level.

- ▶ *Refresh interval.* How often GroupWise checks for new messages (minimum is 1 minute, maximum is 60 minutes and 59 seconds, and the default is 1 minute).

- ▶ *Default action for Sent Items and Attachments.* Establishes what occurs when you double-click on an item in your Sent Items folder or when you double-click on a file attachment. For Sent Items, you can either open the message as it was sent, or view the properties (status information) about the message when you double-click on it. For Attachments, you can either view the attachment using the GroupWise viewers or open the attachment with the associated application.

NOTE

After GroupWise is installed, when you double-click on an item in the Sent Items folder or on a file attachment, a dialog box appears asking you to set the default double-click option. These dialog boxes only appear once. After that, set the double-click action through Options, as explained earlier in this chapter.

Views

Under the Views tab, you can set the following preferences, as shown in Figure 10.3:

- ▶ *Item type.* Select the category (Mail, Phone, Note, Appointment, Task, and Calendar) and the message type (Group or Personal) for which you want to set the default.

- ▶ *Views.* Choose from a list of available views for the selected item type.

- ▶ *Set Default View.* Highlight the view you want as the default for the item type you specify. When you choose File and then New, this is the view that will appear for the message type you choose.

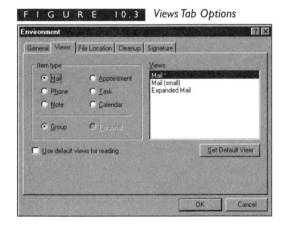

F I G U R E   10.3 *Views Tab Options*

NOTE

The Calendar default view is the view that appears when you select the Calendar View option from the Window menu.

The "Use default views for reading" option enables you to read messages using your default views instead of the views they were sent with. For example, if someone sends you a Small Mail view message, you would normally see the message using the Small Mail view. If you marked the "default views" check box, you would see the message in whichever view you chose as the default.

File Location

Figure 10.4 shows the preferences you can set under the File Location tab.

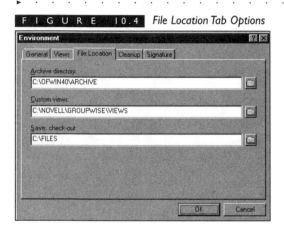

F I G U R E   1 0 . 4   *File Location Tab Options*

- ► *Archive directory.* The location of the *parent* directory of the actual archive directory that holds your archive message files. The system administrator may want you to place your archive files in a certain location.

- ► *Custom views.* The location for Custom View files. Custom views are specialized GroupWise views created with a view designer utility.

- ► *Save, check-out.* The default location for messages and attachments that you save, and the default location to place documents that you check out of a GroupWise library. (See Chapter 8 for more information on using GroupWise libraries.)

Cleanup

Figure 10.5 shows the preferences you can select under the Cleanup tab.

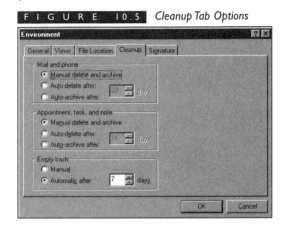

F I G U R E   1 0 . 5   *Cleanup Tab Options*

- ▸ *Mail and phone.* Specifies how old a phone or Mail message will be when it is automatically archived or deleted (minimum is 1 day, maximum is 250 days, and the default is "Manual delete and archive").

- ▸ *Appointment, task, and note.* Specifies how much past Calendar information you want to keep (minimum is 1 day, maximum is 250 days, and the default is "Manual delete and archive").

- ▸ *Empty trash.* Specifies how long any deleted item will stay in the Trash folder (minimum is 1 day, maximum is 250 days, and the default is 7 days).

IMPORTANT

Once messages have been emptied from the Trash folder, they are no longer retrievable.

The options in Cleanup are performed when you exit GroupWise. For example, if you have set Cleanup options so that messages are archived after ten days, the archiving occurs when you exit GroupWise on the tenth day after a message was received. The automatic Cleanup options can cause a slight delay when you exit GroupWise.

Signature

You can enhance your messages with an Internet-style, custom signature. The signature can be added to the end of any message you send. You can include information such as a disclaimer, an encouraging quotation, or your phone number.

To configure a signature, click on the Signature tab in the Environment dialog box, as shown in Figure 10.6.

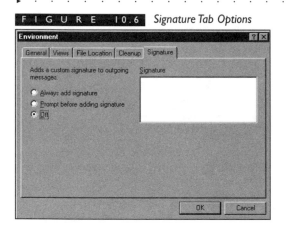

F I G U R E   1 0 . 6 *Signature Tab Options*

- ▸ *Always add signature.* Automatically adds the signature at the end of every message when you click on Send.
- ▸ *Prompt before adding signature.* Asks you if you would like to add a signature when you choose Send. This is the default option.
- ▸ *Off.* Disables the signature function.

Type a signature in the Signature box as you want your signature to appear at the end of messages.

TIP You can copy text into the Clipboard from any application and place it in the Signature box. Graphics and other Rich Text Format (RTF) data cannot be used.

Send

When you double-click on the Send icon, you will see five tabs at the top of the dialog box: Mail/Phone, Appointment, Task, Note, and Advanced, as shown in Figure 10.7. Each tab contains customizable settings that affect the messages you send.

FIGURE 10.7 *The Send Options Dialog Box*

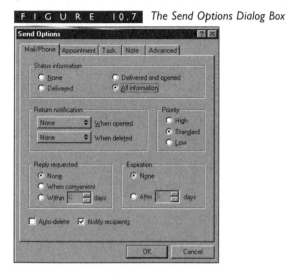

The Mail/Phone, Appointment, Task, and Note tabs contain nearly identical options. The options common to all four tabs are explained in Table 10.1. The options specific to each message type are explained after the table.

T A B L E 10.1	Common Send Options for the Different Message Types	
OPTION	FUNCTION	DETAILS
Status Information	Determines how much information you want to track for each message type.	*None.* No status information will appear in the item properties.
		Delivered. Shows you if and when the message was delivered to the recipient's Mailbox.
		Delivered and Opened. Shows when the message was delivered and when the message was opened.
		All Information. Shows all of the above information, plus information about when the message was deleted, accepted, declined, and so on.
Priority	Determines the default priority for each message type.	*High.* The message appears with a red icon in the recipient's Mailbox, and may be delivered quicker by GroupWise.
		Medium. The message appears with a regular icon in the Mailbox.
		Low. The message appears with a dimmed icon in the Mailbox.

(continued)

Return Notification	Enables you to specify if and how you want to be notified of events triggered by the recipient, such as when the recipient opened, deleted, accepted, declined, or completed the message.	*Mail Receipt.* You receive a Mail message in your Mailbox informing you of the event. *Notify.* You receive an on-screen notification message informing you of the event. *Notify and Mail.* You receive both of the above.
Notify Recipients	Specifies if the recipients receive a Notify message when the message arrives in their Mailboxes.	

You can set message send options on a message-by-message basis. To set Send options for an individual message, open the message window, select File, and then choose Properties.

Mail/Phone, Appointment, and Note Tab Options

Send options that are specific to the Mail/Phone, Appointment, and Note tabs are shown in Table 10.2.

T A B L E 1 0 . 2	Mail/Phone, Appointment, and Note Tab Options	
OPTION	**FUNCTION**	**DETAILS**
Reply Requested	Enables you to inform the recipient that you would like a reply to the message. When you set a Reply Requested option, GroupWise inserts text in the message body, stating that a reply is requested and how soon the reply is desired. The message icon shows two-way arrows, indicating that a reply is requested.	*When Convenient.* Inserts the following text in the message body: `Reply Requested: When Convenient.` *Within X Days.* Inserts the following text in the message body: `Reply Requested: By mm/dd/yy.`
Expiration	Enables you to specify when the message will automatically be deleted from the recipient's Mailbox if the message is not opened.	
Auto-Delete	Automatically removes the message from your Sent Items folder after all recipients have deleted the item and emptied it from their Trash folders.	

Task

The Task tab has one unique option: *Display due date length.* This option enables you to specify whether you want the due date to appear as an ending date (for example, Due on 10/15/1996) or as a length of time (for example, Due in 5 days).

Advanced

The options available under the Advanced tab are shown in Figure 10.8.

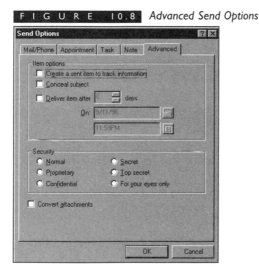

FIGURE 10.8 *Advanced Send Options*

▶ *Create a sent item to track information.* Creates a copy of every item and stores it in the Sent Items folder.

▶ *Conceal subject.* Prevents the message subject line from appearing in the recipient's Mailbox. The subject line only appears when the recipient opens the item. Use this feature as an additional security measure when prying eyes may obtain information simply by seeing the subject line in the Mailbox.

▶ *Deliver item after.* Enables you to create a message now that will be sent after a specified number of days.

▶ *Security.* Enables you to tag your messages with an introductory sentence stating the message security level at the beginning of each message.

WARNING

The Security option under the Advanced tab does *not* in any way place security restrictions on the message; it simply labels the message as having a particular security status.

Security

When you double-click on the safe icon in the Options dialog box, you see the Security Options dialog box. Unlike the Security option under the Advanced Send Options tab (which merely inserts text at the beginning of your messages), the options available in the Security Options dialog box actually affect the security of your messages.

Password

One of the most important Security options is the Password option, shown in Figure 10.9.

F I G U R E   10.9 *Setting a Password*

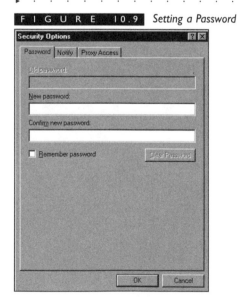

To set a password on your Mailbox:

1. Double-click on the Security icon and click once on the Password tab.
2. If you are changing a password, enter your old password in the Old password: field.
3. Type a password in the New password: field, and in the Confirm new password: field. Choose OK to set the password. The next time you start GroupWise, you will need to type in your password.

IMPORTANT

The password is case-sensitive. Even though it can be reset by the administrator, be sure to record your password somewhere secure.

Click on the "Remember password" box if you don't want to enter your GroupWise password when you start GroupWise. If another person on the network tries to access your Mailbox, the person has to enter your password. As long as you are logged into the network as yourself, you won't have to type it in.

Notify

The Notify tab enables you to use the Notify program, alerting you when you receive a message or when someone else receives a message. You can also be alerted by alarms set in your own Calendar as well as in other peoples' Calendars. As with the Proxy feature, the other person needs to grant you the right to "subscribe to my notifications" or "subscribe to my alarms." See the section called "Using the Proxy Feature" in Chapter 7 for instructions on granting access to your Mailbox.

The Notify tab options are shown in Figure 10.10.

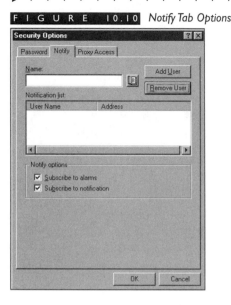

To receive notification when someone else receives a message (or to be alerted for another person's alarms):

1. Click on the Address Book icon to the right of the Name: field. Select a user from the list and choose OK.

2. With that person highlighted in the Notification List, check either the "Subscribe to alarms" or "Subscribe to notification" box. Notice that your name is already on the list.

3. Choose OK to apply your change. Your Notify program will now alert you for messages and/or alarms for both yourself and other users you selected.

Date & Time

The Date & Time icon opens the Date Time Options dialog box, which contains three categories of options: Calendar, Busy Search, and Format.

Calendar

The Calendar options are shown in Figure 10.11.

Calendar Options

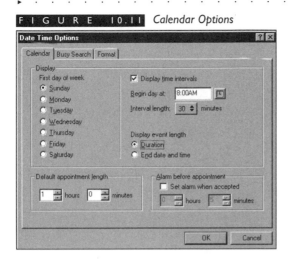

▸ *First day of week.* Enables you to specify which day you want to display as the first day of the week in your Calendar.

▸ *Display time intervals.* Displays the time increments in the Calendar view. If this option is not selected, only the start and end times of your Appointments appear.

▸ *Begin day at.* Sets the starting time for the Appointment list in your Calendar view.

▸ *Interval length.* Specifies the length of the time intervals that appear in your Calendar view.

▸ *Display event length.* Specifies whether you want the event length to appear as a starting and ending time, or as a duration in your Calendar.

▸ *Default appointment length.* Specifies the default duration of the Appointment messages you send.

▸ *Alarm before appointment.* Specifies how much time before your Appointments your alarm should sound.

Busy Search

The Busy Search options are shown in Figure 10.12.

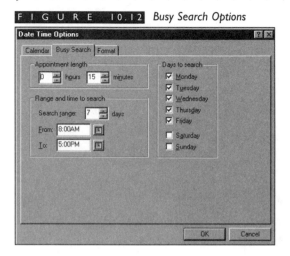

F I G U R E   10.12 *Busy Search Options*

- ▶ *Appointment length.* Specifies the default Appointment length for Appointments you create with the Busy Search feature.

- ▶ *Search range.* Enables you to specify the default number of days that you want to search.

- ▶ *From/To.* Enables you to specify the default time ranges during each day that you want searched.

- ▶ *Days to search.* Enables you to choose the default days you want included in the Busy Search.

Format

The Format tab options enable you to select your preferences for the display of dates and times, as shown in Figure 10.13.

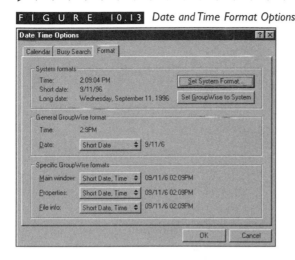

FIGURE 10.13 *Date and Time Format Options*

▸ *System formats.* Enables you to set the default, system time format. This option enables you to access the Windows 95 Regional Settings dialog box.

▸ *General GroupWise format.* Enables you to specify a date and time display format that will be used as the default throughout GroupWise screens.

▸ *Specific GroupWise formats.* Enables you to specify different formats for the GroupWise main window, properties, and file information.

Customizing the Toolbar

You can customize the Toolbar to include the functions and features you use most frequently, and you can arrange them in the order that makes most sense to you.

Toolbars appear in many different GroupWise screens. You have a Toolbar for each message view and for the main GroupWise screen. You can set different options for each.

To customize any Toolbar, right-click on the Toolbar and select Properties. The Toolbar Properties dialog box appears, as shown in Figure 10.14.

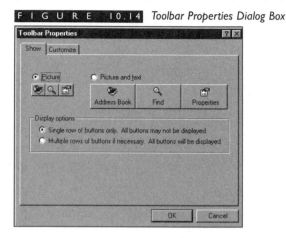

The Show tab enables you to select what should be displayed on the Toolbar — only the picture or both picture and text. You can also specify one or multiple rows.

The Customize tab, shown in Figure 10.15, enables you to specify which GroupWise features appear on the Toolbar.

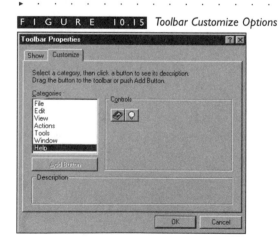

To add a menu option to the Toolbar:

1. Click the category that the feature belongs to, for example, the Tools category contains options for the Address Book and Hit the Road tools.

2. Double-click on the button you want on the Toolbar. The button will appear on the Toolbar, or

3. Click and drag the button to your desired location on the Toolbar.

Customizing Your Folders

In Chapter 4, you saw how to use folders to help organize your messages. By adjusting the properties of the folders in your Mailbox, you can arrange to see folder contents when the folder is opened, see who has access to the messages in the folder (if anyone), and specify what columns are displayed. Each folder can be customized individually. For example, the Mailbox can be set up to display only the Subject: and From: fields, and the Sent Items folder can be set up to display Subject:, Opened status, and Date: fields.

Property Sets

Even though you can set up a "parent/child" folder structure, folder properties are set for each folder individually. These folder properties are grouped into sets:

▶ *General.* Holds general information about the folder such as the owner and description.

▶ *Display.* Configures folder settings to determine how messages are displayed in the folder and what columns are used.

▶ *Sharing.* Determines access to the messages in the folder.

The properties available for folders differ, depending on the folder you are configuring. All folders contain General and Display setting tabs.

The Sent Items and Task List folders include a Find tab. The Trash folder contains a Cleanup property tab.

User-created folders contain a unique tab named Sharing. This tab enables you to share the folders with other GroupWise users.

To display or change the properties of a folder, right-click on the folder and choose Properties.

General Folder Options

Figure 10.16 shows the General folder properties.

► • ◄

F I G U R E   1 0 . 1 6 *General Folder Properties*

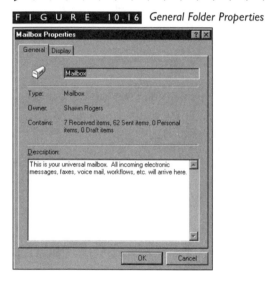

► *Type.* Describes the type of folder — Personal, Calendar, Mailbox, and so forth.

► *Owners.* Specifies the creator of the folder.

► *Contains.* Provides a summary of the folder's contents.

► *Description.* Gives a general description of the folder.

Display Options

Figure 10.17 depicts the Display tab of the Mailbox Properties dialog box.

Mailbox Properties Dialog Box

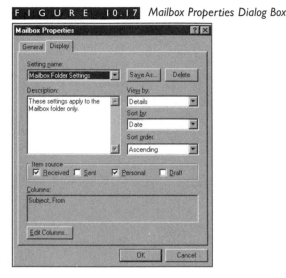

WiseGuide

If you would like to save a custom set of folder settings, click on the Save As button, enter a name for the folder setting, and choose OK. Your new custom set will appear under the Setting Name drop-down list.

► *Setting name.* A drop-down list of preconfigured folder settings.

► *Description.* A description for this group of folder settings.

► *View by.* Sets the display to Message Details, Message Thread, or Calendar formats as the display for the items in this folder.

► *Sort by.* Determines a piece of information about the messages that all messages in this folder will be sorted by (for example, by Date, From, and so on).

► *Sort order.* Ascending or descending display of the items in this folder.

► *Item source.* Tells GroupWise what the originating source is of the messages in this folder — Received, Sent, Personal, or Draft messages.

► *Columns.* Determines which pieces of information will appear in the columns in the Items Area. Choose Edit Columns to add or delete columns.

TIP

Make sure that the piece of information by which you are sorting the messages is also a column.

Sharing

Sharing options for folders determine who has access to the messages inside of them. Chapter 4 discusses how to use shared folders in detail.

Summary

In this chapter, we explained how to make GroupWise work the way you want it to by setting default GroupWise options, customizing your GroupWise Toolbars, and customizing your folders.

GroupWise Startup

The GroupWise Startup screen, shown in Figure A.1, is an introductory screen you see the first time you run the GroupWise client software. After installation of the program, you normally don't see the Startup screen again. (When you double-click on the GroupWise icon, GroupWise simply opens your Mailbox.)

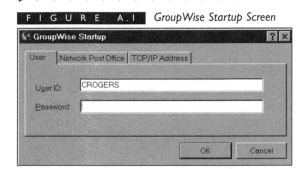

F I G U R E   A . 1   *GroupWise Startup Screen*

Sometimes the GroupWise Startup screen appears if your GroupWise system does not recognize your login ID or GroupWise user ID. In that situation, you are prompted to enter the startup information. The system requires this information in order to locate your stored GroupWise messages on the network.

If the Startup screen appears, the first thing to check is your GroupWise user ID and password. If the correct ID does not appear, type it in and choose OK.

If your user ID is correct, you will need to tell GroupWise how to locate your messages on the network.

Enabling GroupWise to Locate Your Messages

Depending on the configuration of your system, you will need to either

▸ Provide a *mapped drive* to your GroupWise post office, or

▸ Provide the TCP/IP information needed to connect to your Post Office Agent.

(The *GroupWise post office* is the database where your messages are stored on the network. The *Post Office Agent* is a program that handles communication between the GroupWise client program and your GroupWise post office.)

Using a Mapped Drive to the Post Office

If you use a mapped drive to connect to your post office, you must click on the Network Post Office tab and enter the path, such as Y:\GWPOST. You should ask your system administrator whether you use a drive mapping and, if so, what path you should use.

The GroupWise Startup screen with the Network Post Office tab is shown in Figure A.2.

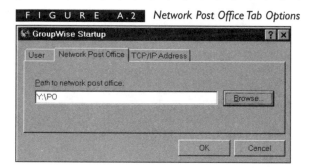

F I G U R E A.2 *Network Post Office Tab Options*

If you are using TCP/IP to connect to your post office in Client/Server mode, you won't need to enter anything in this field. Ask your GroupWise system administrator if you should use Client/Server mode.

Using a TCP/IP Connection to the Post Office

If you connect to the post office via TCP/IP, you need to enter the TCP/IP address of the Post Office Agent and specify a port number. Again, you will need to ask your system administrator what information to enter. (Typically the port number is 1677.)

NOTE To use a TCP/IP connection, your Windows 95 workstation needs to be configured with TCP/IP. See your Windows 95 documentation for information on how to add TCP/IP to your workstation. Your system administrator will need to specify the TCP/IP address for your workstation.

Figure A.3 shows the GroupWise Startup dialog box with the TCP/IP Address tab selected.

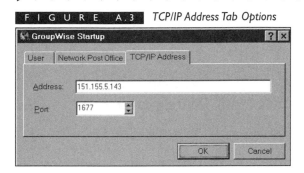

FIGURE A.3 *TCP/IP Address Tab Options*

The TCP/IP address you enter in this dialog box is the address to the Post Office Agent, *not* your workstation's TCP/IP address. The TCP/IP address of the Post Office Agent machine is a requirement for Client/Server access to GroupWise. Your system might not have Client/Server access enabled, in which case you would use the Network Post Office tab to configure a path to your post office.

Connecting to GroupWise

After you enable GroupWise to locate your messages by following the steps in the preceding section, you should be able to log into your GroupWise system. Click on OK.

You will notice a small screen telling you that you are connecting to GroupWise, as shown in Figure A.4.

FIGURE A.4 *Connecting to GroupWise*

If GroupWise still cannot find your Mailbox after you enter a network path or an IP address (usually as a result of a system failure), it will run in Remote Mode. You will still be able to use GroupWise off-line and will be able to send your messages when the system comes back online.

Calling Up the Startup Dialog Box

You can specify that GroupWise bring up the Startup screen every time it launches by simply adding a few characters to the GroupWise startup properties. *Startup properties* are parameters stored with the GroupWise icon that tell GroupWise what to do when it launches. Often, it is necessary to bring up the Startup screen when multiple users run GroupWise from the same computer.

To bring up the GroupWise Startup screen upon launching:

1. Right-click on the GroupWise icon and choose Properties from the menu.

2. Click on the Shortcut tab.

3. Place the cursor in the Target field and go to the end of the command.

4. Add a space, followed by /@u-?, after the GRPWISE.EXE command line. Be sure to include a space between the command line and the / character.

Figure A.5 shows the Properties screen with an example of the proper parameter syntax.

5. Choose OK. The next time you double-click the GroupWise icon, you will see the GroupWise Startup screen.

If you want to create multiple GroupWise icons, one for each person who uses the computer, follow the same steps listed previously, but substitute each user's GroupWise ID in place of the question mark in step 4. (In Windows 95, you can copy an icon by right-clicking on the icon and dragging it to a new location.)

FIGURE A.5   *GroupWise Startup Properties Dialog Box*

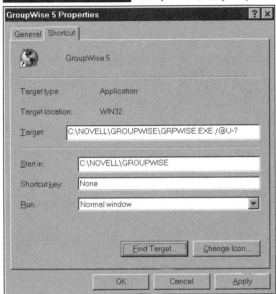

Online Help

If you have read the entire *Novell's GroupWise 5 User's Handbook* and are still uncertain how to perform a function in GroupWise, check the index at the back of the book for topics you may have missed. If you still can't find the answer, you should investigate the GroupWise online help system.

This appendix explains how to use the online help resources available in GroupWise 5.

F1 Key

Press the F1 function key anywhere in GroupWise to get immediate help on the GroupWise feature you are using at that moment.

Help Button

In most dialog boxes, you will find a Help button. Click on this button to view an in-depth explanation of the dialog box or feature that you're using. The help information typically explains options and gives examples of how to use the dialog box.

Toolbar Help

If you allow the mouse pointer to rest for more than a second or two on any Toolbar button, a pop-up window appears, telling you what function the button performs.

Help Menu

The Help menu offers different options depending on the area of GroupWise you're working in. For example, in the main GroupWise screen, the Help menu topics cover general GroupWise issues. If you have the Address Book open, the Help menu provides information about Address Book topics.

Help Topics

In the main GroupWise Screen, the Help Topics option under the Help menu opens the dialog box shown in Figure B.1. You can enter the first few letters of the topic you need help with, and the list will automatically scroll down to that topic.

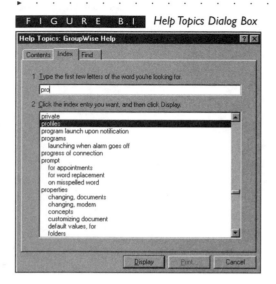

FIGURE B.1 Help Topics Dialog Box

When you have found the topic you want to learn more about, double-click on the topic. The Topics Found dialog box in Figure B.2 appears. Click on the Display button to see the help information.

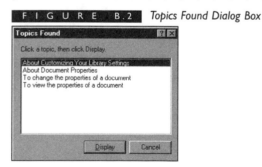

FIGURE B.2 Topics Found Dialog Box

GroupWise Guides

GroupWise Guides are built-in instructional aids that can help you perform certain tasks while GroupWise is running. Although you won't find a Guide for every possible task you can perform in GroupWise, these Guides come in handy when you are getting started with GroupWise.

Unlike some online help systems that simply explain procedures, GroupWise Guides actually lead you through the necessary steps. For example, if you use a Guide to create an Appointment, the Guide will actually create the Appointment as it explains each step.

To access GroupWise Guides, click on the Guides option under the Help menu.

There are six main areas of GroupWise Guides, as shown in Figure B.3.

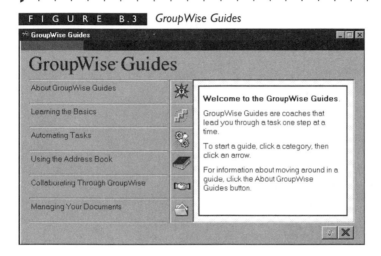

FIGURE B.3 *GroupWise Guides*

About GroupWise Guides teaches you how to use the Guides.

Learning the Basics walks you through the most basic skills in GroupWise, such as setting up an Appointment, retracting items, moving items to folders, and scheduling a recurring event. This guide also offers a "What's New in GroupWise 5" topic that helps GroupWise 4 users transition to GroupWise 5.

Automating Tasks helps you create three rules with the Rules feature: one to handle messages while you're on vacation or away, another to sort mail, and the third to automatically update folders.

Using the Address Book gives you a tour of the Address Book. This guide also walks you through the process of creating a Personal Group and adding a user to your personal address book.

Collaborating Through GroupWise teaches you how to share a document, share a folder, create a discussion group, and manage another person's Mailbox.

Managing Your Documents takes you on a tour of a GroupWise document library, shows you how to create a new document or a new version of an existing document, and explains how to check-out and check-in a document.

In Other Words

The *In Other Words* feature is another handy help tool, located under the Help menu. With the In Other Words option, you can type words or questions that make sense to you, instead of trying to think of obscure keywords. Figure B.4, for example, shows the results of the search when you type Notify and then click on Search.

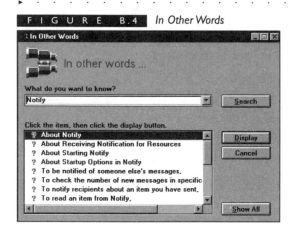

F I G U R E   B.4   *In Other Words*

Double-click on any of the topics to display help information.

Your most recent searches appear in a drop-down list in case you want to reuse or modify a previous search string. To access your previous searches, click on the arrow to the right of the field where you enter your search string.

Link to the Novell Home Page

The Link to the Novell Home Page option launches your Internet browser application (for example, Netscape Navigator) and takes you to the Novell GroupWise home page. The home page provides several helpful GroupWise links to find current information about GroupWise and other Novell products.

About GroupWise

The About GroupWise option opens the window shown in Figure B.5.

FIGURE B.5 *About GroupWise*

This information is helpful when you are troubleshooting in GroupWise. From this window you can determine which version of GroupWise you're running, the release date, where you are running GroupWise from (your hard drive or the network), your user name, your file ID (an ID used to identify your Mailbox files on the network), the name of the GroupWise post office you are connected to, the path to the post office (if you are using a drive-mapped connection), and the IP address you are using to connect to the post office (if you are running in Client/Server mode).

Internet Features

Sending Messages over the Internet

You can use GroupWise to send and receive e-mail over the Internet, as long as the proper groundwork has been put in place. The groundwork involves configuring your GroupWise system's link to the Internet so messages can pass to and from the Internet. Your GroupWise system administrator should handle this configuration.

For the purposes of this appendix, assume that your GroupWise system has been configured with the following:

- A connection to the Internet
- A registered Internet address for your company (for example, acme.com)
- A GroupWise domain named INTERNET (a *domain* is the part of your GroupWise system that handles the administration of messages)
- An SMTP gateway to transfer messages to and from the Internet

You can use GroupWise to send e-mail messages over the Internet to anyone with an Internet connection, including users who have accounts with Internet Service Providers (ISPs) and people at other companies that use different e-mail systems.

Because the messages in GroupWise are formatted in a way that is unique to GroupWise, your messages need to be translated into a universal format before they can be sent over the Internet. This common format is called Simple Mail Transfer Protocol (SMTP).

Remember that not all of the GroupWise message types will be understood or supported by the receiving e-mail system. For example, if you send an Appointment invitation to someone who does not have GroupWise, that person will receive the message as a regular e-mail message. Always keep the recipient's e-mail system in mind when you are sending messages over the Internet.

Addressing Internet Mail

The GroupWise addresses you use for Internet e-mail need to be converted to the proper format before your messages can be delivered to people over the Internet.

A standard Internet address has this format:

user@domain.com

The user portion of the address refers to an individual you are sending e-mail to. The domain.com portion refers to the registered Internet domain name for the person's company or ISP. (Other types of Internet addresses have different extensions at the end, such as .org and .edu.)

Here is an example of an Internet e-mail address:

rmctague@acme.com

Once you know the Internet address of the person you want to communicate with, you need to use the proper GroupWise Internet address format.

In our example, the system administrator has set up a GroupWise domain named ACME. From our GroupWise system, we simply open up a new Mail message and place the address in the To: field like this:

INTERNET:rmctague@acme.com

When the message is sent, GroupWise sends the message to the proper GroupWise domain through an SMTP gateway. The gateway converts the message to SMTP format, and uses the rmctague@acme.com portion of the address to route the message over the Internet.

You can store people's Internet addresses in a personal address book. (See Chapter 3 for more information about personal address books.)

Sending Internet File Attachments

SMTP, the standard format for e-mail messages sent over the Internet, is not capable of handling file attachments to messages. Given the increased use of the Internet for multimedia (such as sound and voice) data, people needed some way to create file attachments to transmit different kinds of files over the Internet. Therefore, Multipurpose Internet Mail Extension (MIME) attachments were developed.

Because the GroupWise SMTP gateway supports MIME attachments, you can attach most any type of file to your messages. When a file attachment reaches a recipient's e-mail system, it should still be intact — regardless of the e-mail system the recipient uses. (However, the receiving mail system must support MIME as well.)

Creating Internet Address Messages

Suppose you are surfing the Internet's World Wide Web and you run across a site that you know a friend would be interested in. With GroupWise 5, you can send an Internet Address message to that person. An *Internet Address message* lists the Uniform Resource Locator (URL) for any Web site you want to share with someone else.

NOTE

In order to view World Wide Web pages, you need a Web browser, such as Netscape Navigator.

To send an Internet Address message:

1. Click on Tools and then choose Internet.
2. Choose Send Internet Location. You'll see the dialog box shown in Figure C.1.

FIGURE C.1 *Send Internet Location Dialog Box*

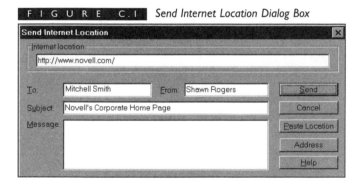

3. In the Internet Location field, enter the URL (or paste it from the Windows Clipboard).
4. Address the message as you would any other GroupWise message and then choose Send.

When the recipient opens the message, a button named Go to Location appears. If the recipient clicks on the button, the recipient's Web browser will launch automatically and go directly to the Web site.

Using Internet References

You can store URLs in a GroupWise folder as references. (See Chapter 8 for more information on references.) This practice enables you to access your favorite Web pages straight from GroupWise.

To create a reference to a Web site:

1. Highlight the folder where you would like the reference to appear.

2. Click on Tools, Internet, and Create Internet Location. The dialog box shown in Figure C.2 appears.

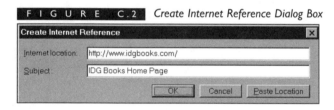

F I G U R E   C.2   *Create Internet Reference Dialog Box*

3. Enter the Internet address in the Internet Location field.

4. Enter a description of the location in the Subject: field.

5. Click on OK.

A reference to the Web site appears in the selected folder. To access the Web site, simply double-click on the reference.

NOTE   Internet Address messages are a feature of GroupWise 5.0 only. In GroupWise 5.1 URLs entered in the body of a regular Mail message are automatically converted into hypertext links.

GroupWise Remote Mode Worksheet

Use this worksheet to record the configuration information needed to set up GroupWise in Remote Mode.

User Information

Full name _____

User ID _____

Password _____

System Information

Domain _____

Post Office _____

Network Connection

Path to Post Office _____

TCP/IP Connection

TCP/IP address of the
GroupWise Mail Server _____

Port address _____

Modem Connection

Gateway Login ID _____

Gateway password _____

Phone number _____

Time Zone _____

Overview of the 16-Bit GroupWise 5 Client

In this appendix, you will learn about the GroupWise 16-bit client interface. The 16-bit version of the GroupWise client is designed to run on 16-bit operating systems.

What is the difference between 16-bit and 32-bit operating systems? Using an analogy of a highway is the easiest way to explain the difference. The 16-bit operating system has 16 lanes of traffic (or data), and the 32-bit operating system has 32 lanes of traffic (or data). A 16-bit operating system cannot run programs that are written to run on a 32-bit operating system.

NOTE A 16-bit application can run on a 32-bit operating system such as Windows 95 or Windows NT, but the 32-bit version of the application is preferable for the 32-bit environment.

Comparison of the 16-Bit and 32-Bit Clients

There are three main areas where the 16-bit version of GroupWise 5 differs from the 32-bit version: performance, folder structure, and features.

Performance

Depending upon your system, the 16-bit client may actually be faster than the 32-bit version. The 16-bit client may be faster due to the program size and because it was the original client that was created for GroupWise. If you are running Windows 3.1 or Windows for Workgroups, the 16-bit client is your only option.

If you are running Windows 95 or Windows NT 4.0, you can use either version of the GroupWise client. However, because there are certain features in the 32-bit client that are not available in the 16-bit client, the 32-bit client is usually preferable.

Folder Structure

Because of the interface differences, the folder structure in the 16-bit client differs slightly from what you see in the 32-bit client. Figure E.1 shows a folder structure in the 32-bit client.

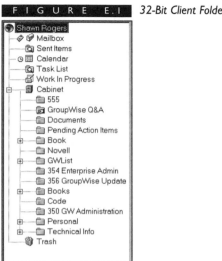

Figure E.2 shows the same folder structure in the 16-bit client.

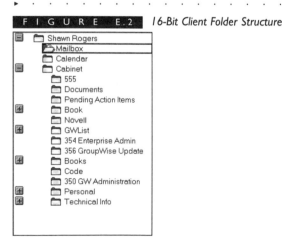

Table E.1 lists the folders you see in the 32-bit client and explains how they are accessed in the 16-bit client.

TABLE E.1 *Comparison of Folders in 32-Bit and 16-Bit Clients*

32-BIT CLIENT	16-BIT CLIENT
Mailbox Folder	In Box and Out Box, accessed through icons in the GroupWise main screen
Sent Items Folder	Out Box
Calendar Folder	Calendar folders in the In Box and Out Box and Calendar views, accessed through the calendar icon in the main screen
To Do Folder	Task List in My Calendar view, accessed through the calendar icon in the main screen and the Calendar folders in the In Box and Out Box
Cabinet Folder	In Box and Out Box
Folders Under Cabinet	Folders found under the In Box and Out Box Cabinet folders
Trash Folder	Trash window, accessed through the Trash icon in the GroupWise main screen
Work In Progress Folder	No equivalent

The 32-bit client does not have an In Box, Out Box, or Trash icon. In the 32-bit client, these 16-bit features are combined in a single interface.

Features

For the most part, you can do the same tasks with the 16-bit client as you can with the 32-bit client. The major exceptions are listed below, based on the status of GroupWise at the time of this writing:

▶ *Shared Folders.* The capability to share folders among GroupWise users has not been implemented in the 16-bit client.

▶ *Work In Progress Folder.* The capability to automatically save messages in a work-in-progress state has not been implemented in the 16-bit client.

▶ *Access to Document Libraries.* The document management features available in the 32-bit client are not available in the 16-bit client.

▶ *Personal Address Books.* The 16-bit client Address Book does not enable you to create personal address books.

Using the 16-Bit Client

The 16-bit client of GroupWise 5 provides most of the same functionality as its 32-bit counterpart; however, the 16-bit client runs on computers using Microsoft Windows 3.11 or Windows for Workgroups (both 16-bit operating systems).

All GroupWise users, regardless of their computing platform, use common message formats. For example, someone using the 16-bit version of the GroupWise client can schedule meetings with other people who may be using the Macintosh, 32-bit, or UNIX client.

Because the message format is always the same, each client platform can "translate" the information and display it in the recipient's native computing environment. When you send messages to people with different computing platforms, you don't have to know how to use the various operating systems those people are running.

When you open the GroupWise 16-bit client, the main screen appears automatically. You can access all of the messaging features of GroupWise from the main screen, shown in Figure E.3.

F I G U R E   E.3   *16-Bit Client Main Screen*

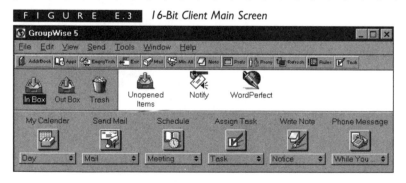

In GroupWise, the main screen does not function like screens in other Windows applications. When you maximize the main screen, it does not expand to fill the entire screen. Rather, the Shelf (discussed later) expands to allow room for more icons. You use the main screen to access other windows, such as the In Box, the Out Box, and the Trash. These other windows *can* be maximized to fill the entire screen.

In GroupWise, you can perform the same functions in a number of ways (for example, opening the Calendar or reading your Mail). Often, there are many ways to do the same thing — whether you prefer to use icons, menus, or QuickMenus.

TIP The programmers at Novell have finally found a good use for the right-hand button on your mouse: QuickMenus. Wherever you are in the GroupWise 16-bit client, you can press the right mouse button to display options for that area, as shown in Figure E.4. For example, if you are looking at your folders, you can click on the right mouse button to see a menu of options related to folders.

FIGURE E.4 A QuickMenu

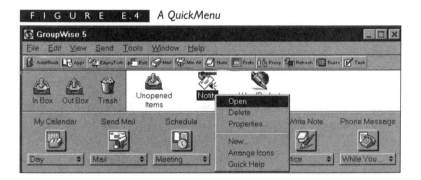

The GroupWise 16-bit interface consists of four main parts: the pull-down menus, the animated icons, the Shelf, and the action buttons.

Pull-Down Menus

Similar to other Windows 3.x applications, the GroupWise 16-bit client contains pull-down menus that can be used to access the features of the various screens. Often, you can use different methods to access the same features. For example, to send a Mail message, you can click on the Send menu and then choose New Mail. Alternatively, you can simply double-click on the Send Mail action button.

The Animated Icons

The animated icons in the GroupWise 16-bit interface are the In Box icon and the Trash icon, as shown in Figure E.5. These icons are called *animated icons* because their appearance changes to reflect different conditions.

F I G U R E   E.5   *Animated Icons*

Animated Icons

NOTE The Out Box icon is not really an animated icon because its appearance never changes. However, we discuss the Out Box icon because all three icons have been grouped together in the GroupWise main screen.

The In Box

When you want to see your new messages, you must open the In Box. When you receive a new message, an unopened envelope icon appears in the In Box, as shown in Figure E.6.

You open the In Box by double-clicking on it. You will see a list of your opened and unopened mail.

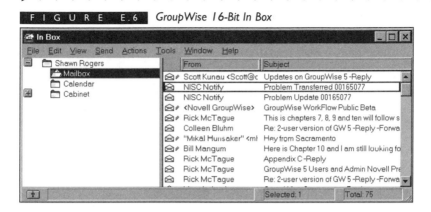

To read a message, simply double-click on the message line. The text portion of the message will appear. The In Box also contains folders, where you can organize your messages. Folders can be used to organize messages the same way you use the directory and subdirectory structure in the Windows File Manager to organize files. You can place messages that pertain to the same project in a folder, you can nest folders under each other, and you can link a message to multiple folders.

The 16-bit version of the GroupWise client does not support shared folders at the time of this writing.

NOTE

The Out Box

Use the Out Box to manage messages you have sent. When you open the Out Box, you will notice that it looks very similar to the In Box. The difference is that the In Box contains your incoming mail and the Out Box contains the messages you have sent. The Out Box enables you to perform three very handy tasks: viewing the status of the messages you have sent, resending a message, and retracting a message that has already been sent (provided it has not been opened yet). Figure E.7 shows an open Out Box.

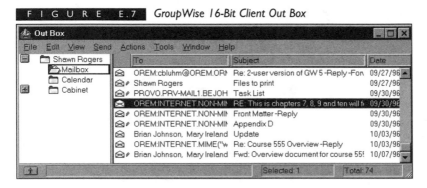

The same folders you see in your In Box appear in the Out Box, so you can organize your outgoing messages the same way you organize your incoming messages. When you double-click on a sent message, you will see complete status information for the message, including when the message was delivered, opened, deleted, completed (if the message was a task), forwarded, accepted, or declined (if the message was an Appointment).

When the Out Box is open, you can resend messages that have not been received. To resend a message, select the Resend option from the Send menu. When you edit and resend a message, you can retract the original message as long as it hasn't been opened yet. If you want to retract a message you have sent, highlight the message in the Out Box and press the Delete key. Select Delete from All Mailboxes. This process will delete the message from the recipients' In Boxes, as well as from your own Out Box.

You can only retract e-mail messages that have not been opened.

IMPORTANT

Trash

When you delete a message from your In Box, your Out Box, or your Calendar, the message goes into the Trash and a mound of trash appears in the Trash icon on your screen.

In Windows 3.x, you can click on the Trash icon and drag it to your desktop for easy access.

TIP

To view the messages in the Trash, simply double-click on the Trash icon. Figure E.8 shows what the Trash looks like when it is open.

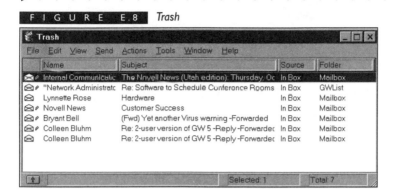

F I G U R E   E . 8 *Trash*

There are basically two functions associated with the Trash: undeleting messages and emptying the Trash.

If you decide you want to retrieve a deleted message from the Trash, simply highlight the message, choose Edit, and then select Undelete. The message will then be restored to its original location in the In Box, the Out Box, or the Calendar.

To empty the Trash, choose Edit and then Empty Trash. This purges all deleted messages from your Mailbox. The messages emptied from the Trash are *permanently* deleted. You cannot undelete a message after it has been emptied from the Trash.

Messages are automatically emptied from the Trash after seven days. However, you can choose Preferences from the File menu to adjust the number of days that deleted messages stay in the Trash before they are automatically removed.

The Shelf

The Shelf is similar to a Windows 3.x Program Group. You can create icons and place them on the Shelf so you can easily access Windows programs from the GroupWise main screen, as shown in Figure E.9. The Shelf feature can really help you use GroupWise more effectively — you can retrieve messages, view your Calendar, and launch applications all from the same screen. Shortcuts to different GroupWise features can also be added to the Shelf area.

FIGURE E.9 *The Shelf*

The Shelf

The icons on the Shelf are similar to Windows Program Items. To view the properties of a Shelf icon, press Alt and Enter at the same time. You can then modify the icon. For example, you can change the icon's name or add information to the command line. To add an icon to the Shelf, go to the File menu and choose New. Enter the command line for the program whose icon you want to add.

Here is a quick way to add icons to the Shelf: open File Manager, click on an executable file, and drag it to the Shelf.

TIP

Action Buttons

Action buttons are an easy way to create e-mail messages, Appointments, Tasks, Notes, and Phone messages. You can also use action buttons to view your Calendar. Each action button has two parts: a pop-up list and an icon. The action buttons are shown in Figure E.10.

Action Buttons

Action Buttons

The action button pop-up list shows the available views for the screen. *Views* are simply display formats for the different parts of the GroupWise client interface. For example, the Send Mail action button has three views associated with it: Mail, Expanded Mail, and Small Mail. (In the Expanded Mail view, you see a larger-than-normal message area.) To see a list of the views for each action button, click on the list at the bottom of the action button and hold down the mouse button. As you drag the mouse, different views will be highlighted. To choose a view, simply release the mouse button while the view is highlighted.

If the view you want is already displayed on the pop-up list, simply double-click on the action button's icon to open the screen.

The GroupWise client has six action buttons: My Calendar, Send Mail, Schedule, Assign Task, Write Note, and Phone Message.

My Calendar

The Calendar keeps track of your Appointments, Tasks, and Notes. (These message types are explained in the following subsections.) Use the My Calendar action button to view the Calendar.

There are a number of different views for the Calendar. Each view focuses on a different part of the Calendar. The Day view, shown in Figure E.11, is a useful way to look at the Calendar. Other views include Day Planner, Week at a Glance, Notebook, and Deskpad. You can select the view that works best for you.

Day View of a Calendar

The last view you use in the Calendar will automatically appear on My Calendar's pop-up list when you return to the main screen.

TIP

Send Mail

The *Send Mail action button* is the fastest way to create and send e-mail messages. There are three standard views associated with Send Mail: Mail, Small Mail, and Expanded Mail. The Expanded Mail view has a larger message area than the Mail view. The Small Mail view has a smaller message area. Figure E.12 shows the Small Mail view.

Small Mail View

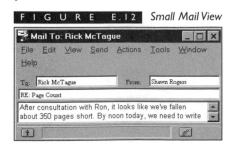

For most screens in this book, the standard Mail view has been used.

Schedule

The *Schedule action button* enables you to send Appointments. There are two different kinds of Appointments you can create: Personal Appointments and Meeting messages.

Personal Appointments are recorded on your own personal Calendar. These Appointments are for your reference only and do not appear on other people's Calendars. Personal Appointments are time-management tools that help you keep track of your daily appointments. Figure E.13 shows an example of a Personal Appointment.

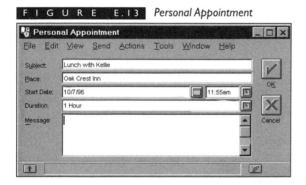

F I G U R E   E.13 *Personal Appointment*

If you want to set up an appointment with someone else, you should create a *Meeting message*. (You can also use Meeting messages to let people know about meetings without actually inviting those people.)

Assign Task

A *Task* is a message type that can be used to manage, prioritize, and delegate projects and duties. Each Task contains a start date, an end date, and a priority rating. Figure E.14 shows an example of one kind of Task, a Personal Task.

Tasks are displayed in Task Lists, which are part of the Calendar. A *Task List* is simply an electronic version of a checklist. Tasks on a Task List carry over from one day to the next if the Tasks have not been marked completed. You can delegate a Task by sending it to someone else, or you can create a *Personal Task* for your own reference.

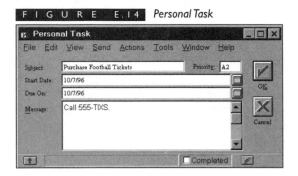

FIGURE E.14 *Personal Task*

Write Note

The *Write Note action button* can be used to create a Note. In GroupWise, *Notes* are the electronic version of Post-it Notes. You can attach a Note to the Calendar to remind yourself to do something. For example, you can use a Note to remind yourself that a project is due on a certain day or that you need to pick up milk on the way home from work. Figure E.15 shows an example of a Personal Note.

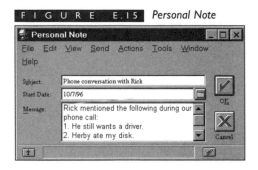

FIGURE E.15 *Personal Note*

You can send Notes to other people as reminders, or you can create Personal Notes for your own Calendar.

Phone Message

A *Phone Message* is an electronic version of the preprinted forms many receptionists use to keep track of telephone messages. In addition to regular

Phone messages, which include information about the person who called, there is a message type called *While You Were Out,* which enables you to designate a priority level to the message. Figure E.16 shows a typical While You Were Out message.

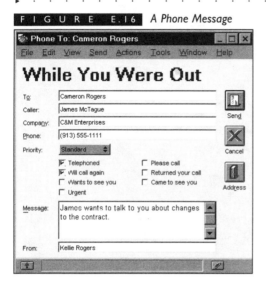

FIGURE E.16 *A Phone Message*

You can create and send Phone messages much the same way you send e-mail messages.

Address Book

When you send messages with the GroupWise 16-bit client, you must access your system's Address Book to address messages. The *Address Book* is a key component of GroupWise. You can use the Address Book to:

- ▶ Address GroupWise messages
- ▶ Access public groups
- ▶ Create personal groups
- ▶ Look up information about other GroupWise users

The Address Book is shown in Figure E.17.

F I G U R E   E . 1 7   *GroupWise 16-Bit Client Address Book*

Addressing Messages with the Address Book

To address messages using the Address Book, from the main GroupWise screen:

1. Double-click on the action button that corresponds to the type of message you want to send and then click on the Address button. Don't forget to first adjust the pop-up list on the action button if necessary.

2. Begin typing the name of the person you want to send the message to. The list of people in your Address Book will automatically scroll forward in response to the letters you type.

3. Double-click on a recipient's name if you want to place it in the To: field, or click and drag names to the To:, CC:, or BC: fields. (The recipients' e-mail addresses will be inserted in the appropriate fields.)

4. Click on OK when you have entered all of the recipients' names in the address fields. The necessary addressing information will automatically be placed into the message.

Accessing Public Groups

Public groups are lists of people who belong to certain departments or workgroups. For example, all members of the Sales Department could be placed into a public group called "Sales." To send a message to all Sales employees, you would simply type Sales in the To: field.

To use the Address Book to send a message to all members of a public group:

1. Click on the Address button in the Mail message and click on the Public Groups button.

2. Double-click on the desired group to move the group into the To: field.

3. Click on OK and the proper addressing information will automatically be placed into the message.

Creating and Using Personal Groups

Unlike public groups, which must be defined by the system administrator, you can create your own *personal groups*. Personal groups enable you to send messages to specific groups of individuals. You decide who will be included in each group. For example, if you work with several coworkers on a certain project, you could create a personal group called "Project" that contains all of those people. When you want to send a message to all members of that group, you would simply type Project in the To: field.

To create a personal group:

1. Open the Address Book and insert the group members' names in the To:, CC:, and BC: fields of an e-mail message.

2. Click on Save Group and type the name of the group.

3. Click on OK to save the personal group.

To send a message to the members of a personal group, type the name of the group in the To: field, or:

1. Open the Address Book and click on Personal Groups.

2. Double-click on the group you want (or highlight the group and choose Retrieve and then Edit).

3. Click on OK and the personal group will automatically appear in the To: field.

Because a personal group can consist of a single person, you can create separate personal groups for people that have long e-mail addresses. For example, if you must enter Internet:boris@russia.gov in the To: field in order to send messages to Boris, you could create a personal group named "Boris" that includes only Boris. Then you would not need to enter Boris's entire address each time you send him a message. You could simply use the personal group name.

To create a personal group for someone on the Internet:

1. Type the person's complete address in the To: field (or open a message you have received from that person and click on Reply).

2. Click on the Address button. The Address Book will open and the address will be listed in the To: field of the Address Book screen.

3. Click on Save Group, and name the personal group that will consist of one person.

4. Click on OK.

Index

B

D

T

priority levels for, 80, 92
receiving, 94–95
rescheduling, 83
retracting, 94
rules and, 103
sending, 91–92
Task tab, 183, 187
TCP/IP Connection dialog box, 169
TCP/IP (Transmission Control
  Protocol/Internet Protocol), 3,
  151, 157, 167–169
telephone integration program, 35,
  46
terminators, 60, 62, 63
threading, message, 58, 117–118
Time Zone button, 160
Time Zone settings, 153, 155–156,
  160–161
To: field, 22–23, 28–29, 38–41, 87
Toolbar, 11–12, 81
  basic description of, 4
  default settings, 193–195
Toolbar Properties dialog box,
  193–195
Tools menu, 104, 108–109, 152,
  164, 167, 170
Transferred message status, 65–66
Trash, 5, 10–11, 30–31, 196
  default settings, 181
  emptying, 68–69
  restoring deleted messages from,
    31, 68
Type property, 196

W

Y

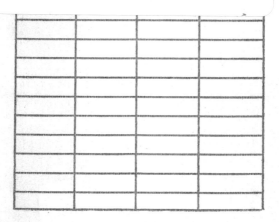